I0048692

"Venture-backed startups operate in a league of their own, fraught with distinct hurdles and high stakes. As a serial entrepreneur and having invested in over 100 startups, I've seen the same pattern: brilliant innovators struggling under the weight of leadership. Peak OS provides a guide for any VC-backed CEO to align their team, master the basics, and drive towards success."

—**SAM YAGAN**, Managing Director Corazon Capital, Co-Founder of SparkNotes & OkCupid, Former CEO of MTCH

"I hate book blurbs (see my blog). That said, if Jeff's passion for helping CEO/founders equals the energy he put into this book, it will be a great read."

—**BRAD FELD**, Partner at Foundry, author of *Venture Deals* and *Startup Boards*

"Techstars has a handful of tried and true criteria for selecting our investments, and the first three are team, team, team! Put simply, we invest in unstoppable founders who are part of unstoppable teams. With *Peak Teams*, Jeff powerfully explains the habits that drive amazing teams like these."

—**DAVID COHEN**, Co-Founder and Chairman at Techstars

"As a former operator and someone that's coached countless startups, Jeff Martin's been there. He understands the inflection points that every VC-backed company traverses, and he's come up with an executable OS that caters to them. Being a startup founder will always be hard, but Jeff's methodology makes the journey easier to navigate."

—**JANINE DAVIS**, Managing Partner and
Executive Coach at Evolution

"Jeff's framework for helping founders succeed is truly unique. He's supported many of the founders that I've backed and have set them up for long-term success."

—**JENNY FIELDING**, Co-Founder and Managing
Director of Everywhere Ventures

"Jeff has crafted the definitive playbook for CEOs of high-stakes, venture-backed companies. While I had the privilege of learning directly from the GOAT Coach of Silicon Valley, Bill Campbell, Jeff's work is rooted in a similar ethos. What's timeless is that a TEAM with great fundamentals wins games...*Peak Teams* shows the way. I strongly recommend that you read this!"

—**MICHAEL MOE**, Founder Global Silicon Valley

"*Peak Teams* is a practical guide for CEOs and teams navigating the complex terrain of entrepreneurial businesses and their teams. With a focus on clear communication, regular cadences, and fostering a culture of learning, Martin offers a systematic approach to help organizations achieve their goals effectively. This book provides a roadmap for turning good teams into exceptional ones."

—**MATT HULETT**, CEO of PedMeds, author of *Unlock*, former President of Rosetta Stone

"Jeff's extensive history with startups has given him a firsthand look at their highs and lows. Recognizing the unique needs of high-growth ventures, he's crafted a different operating model for them. As both a founder and investor, I value his pragmatic, actionable approach in this book. It's a great read for anyone leading startup teams."

—**CAREY RANSOM**, Managing Director at BankTech Ventures, Founder at Operate

PEAK TEAMS

MASTERING THE HABITS OF UNSTOPPABLE VENTURE-BACKED COMPANIES

JEFF JAMES MARTIN

Collective Genius 》》

PEAK TEAMS
Mastering the Habits of Unstoppable Venture-Backed Companies
First Edition

ISBN   978-1-962341-14-1   *Hardcover*
       978-1-962341-13-4   *Paperback*
       978-1-962341-15-8   *Ebook*

For my grandfather, James Nicoloff—a founder I never met, yet one of the most profound influences in my life.

CONTENTS

INTRODUCTION

"The strength of the team is each individual member.
The strength of each member is the team."
—PHIL JACKSON

The lobby erupted in cheers all around me as our founder, Doug Berg, walked into the makeshift conference hall.

It was my first day at techies.com. I'd been hired right out of college because, back in the early days of the dot-com world, VC-backed CEOs were starving for eager talent that understood the all-hands-on-deck nature of an early-stage company. In school, I had double majored in Entrepreneurship and Finance, which had given me a direct knowledge pipeline of tools, systems, and methodologies I funneled directly into my first business, which I was already running. After graduating, I sold that first company, and I felt like I understood the basics of running a business—so I went looking for innovators doing things bigger, faster, and on another level.

I found it at techies. Only a couple of hours into my first day, it felt like drinking from a fire hose. I could tell I had walked into an environment that was *nothing* like the one school had prepared me for.

I'd had the serendipitous luck to be starting work on the day of a company Town Hall, and now, I was standing in a large crowd of my new teammates. Over 200 people were squeezed into the lobby of our already-overcrowded office space; the company was in a serious growth phase, and the building was bursting at the seams. The palpable energy in the room heightened my own excitement.

Doug made a series of announcements, each punctuated by an enthusiastic cheer from the crowd. "We had a record-level quarter!" "We broke all our sales records!"

As he announced the territory sales of each group, they'd erupt into cheers team by team. When he announced Southern California, my own team started chanting, *SO-CAL! SO-CAL!*

The Town Hall concluded with our CEO, Dan Frawley, announcing that we'd just secured one of our most important partnerships. "This puts us into a strategic position—we'll be able to offer value unlike any of our competitors, and we'll need to stay focused to hold our lead."

Dan had been a fighter pilot in a past career, so what he said next carried a lot of weight. "We have to move fast. We have to take calculated moves and follow through. We're building the plane while we're flying it, everyone. Let's make sure we stay in the air."

The response was immediate: the loudest cheer yet. It was energy like I'd never felt before. After the meeting was over, we all rushed back to our desks with only one thing on our minds—the determination to succeed. We were bringing to market an incredible innovation, a product that had never existed before. We had no roadmap, but we knew that if the company won, we would all win too.

The business had been infused with a large Series B raise, so the pace we were able to move at was stunning, and unlike the more measured movement at my previous companies. If those companies were commercial jets—big, powerful, carrying the most people possible from point A to point B—techies. com was an F-18 Super Hornet. I could tell that the VC-backed world was completely different: high stakes, almost no room for failure, and most companies didn't make it. But those that did win, won *big*. (Case in point: techies.com went from $1 million ARR to $35 million ARR in just 18 months.)

As I moved through the first few months of my work with techies, I found myself analyzing and writing down in my head all the behaviors and characteristics of the company. I was like a scientist out in the field observing a particularly fascinating subject. I wanted to answer a burning question that had formed from the moment I felt the new energy at this company: What makes those few winning VC-backed companies succeed, and so many others fail?

Twenty years later, this book is the answer to that question.

UNSTOPPABLE TEAMS

I have a hard time answering the age-old question: "So, what is it that you do?"

I have such a hard time answering it, in fact, that I recently plugged in all my work activities to ChatGPT and asked it to *tell me what I am.* (Unsurprisingly, I didn't get a very useful answer.)

The best way to describe myself is simple: I'm a coach. I always have been. For twenty years, I've coached teams, both in business and in real life. An avid athlete from the moment I could hold a hockey stick, and now a black belt in Brazilian Jiu Jitsu, I've coached hockey, wrestling, BJJ, and watched countless kids level up what they're bringing to the game. With every ounce of improvement, their team benefits; and that's my goal. I'm a coach of teams, not individuals. The same is true for businesses. There are plenty of executive coaches out there; I focus on teams. Helping a team understand how to work together smoothly and bring on results they'd previously thought were out of reach is incredibly satisfying.

So why do I cringe when I hear the words *business coach?* Well, mostly because it brings to mind the image of someone trying to sell stuff online after taking a course from someone else who's trying to sell stuff online. Or I think about someone throwing down a couple thousand for an online "coaching certificate", then opening up shop with no actual experience and empathy for these businesses. The business coaching world has an oversaturation problem, and the careful, methodical, and results-driven work I've done with hundreds of companies over the past two decades is fundamentally different from what I see other business coaches offering.

For the purposes of this book, though, there's no better way to describe what I do. I'm a coach. And I help companies build unstoppable teams.

Part of why this is such exciting work, and why I've done it nonstop for twenty years, is that each new company I work with, each team I help find their rhythm and get in a groove, teaches me something new I can impart to the *next* team. It feels like getting a masterclass each and every time I work with a new team.

The Peak Operating System (Peak OS) you'll learn in this book is the result of two decades of working with hundreds of CEOs, founders, leadership teams, and investors in my effort to answer my own question: *What makes VC-backed companies successful?*

As a VC-backed Founder/CEO, that question is probably one you ask yourself every day.

THE CEO STRESS SPIRAL

Taking on starting a business and making it successful is almost an impossible task. Level that up to what VC-backed companies are doing, and it's like landing on the moon.

Venture-backed companies are just *different.* Venture-backed leadership teams face a unique landscape of challenges and opportunities, and it's because these companies are innovators. They're navigating uncharted territory with no roadmap. They're doing something that's never been done before, building something revolutionary. Their mission is more than making a profit; they want to carve out a new sector of the market—or even create a whole new one.

The CEOs of these companies face pressure from above, below, and all sides as they work toward growing the business. They answer to their board; they answer to their teams; they answer to their clients and stakeholders. It's a lot of juggling and keeping various groups of people happy, focused, and clear on their mission.

In my career as a CEO Founder and business coach, I've been privileged to work alongside VC-backed CEOs every day, and in all that time, the most common challenge I hear from them hasn't changed.

It feels like everything is on my shoulders.

The amount of stress and, at times, doubt I hear from these undeniably successful leaders may not surprise you, and probably feels familiar. It's not imposter syndrome; you know you're where you belong. But the sheer number of responsibilities a CEO Founder is juggling would make anyone feel some doubt about sustaining that success.

We're not growing fast enough.

We're struggling to raise capital.

Are we going to be able to live up to the promise I sold the investors?

I really want to make the right choices, but everyone disagrees on what they are.

I'm not sure we have the right people on the team.

I don't know how much to share with the board—what if we share too much, or possibly not enough?

I'm not sure I can pull this off.

Everyone who has read *The E-Myth* knows the mantra, "Work on your business, not in your business." But VC-backed CEOs have to do both. They're the central hub that connects all the spokes of the business: the board, the investors, the clients, the team. It's up to them to make sure the wheel is turning and there's no stick in the spokes jamming up the company's momentum.

If you're reading this and can relate to how it feels, then I wrote this book for you.

What you have in your hands is the key to getting the company off your shoulders. It's the way to get control of how you're operating. It's the way out of the stress spiral. You'll want to give each member of your leadership team a copy of this book; by doing so, you're going to empower them to become unstoppable.

MASTERING THE FUNDAMENTALS

If CEOs are visionaries, then VC-backed CEOs are visionaries where the original map doesn't even exist. It's a whole new level of vision.

I've heard people say that it's the CEO's job to stay focused on vision, but I don't agree with that. CEOs *also* have to understand what their teams are doing and how they're doing it, or they can't effectively make decisions that drive the company forward. They need to know what the day-to-day details are in order to lead their team.

However, CEOs don't have time to have their hand in all the details at all times. When I work with companies, I often see that CEOs are drained by the constant scoping in and scoping out from big vision to on-the-ground details. It takes a lot of mental energy to zoom yourself from a roadmap three quarters out to a set of small decisions that need to be made *today*.

I sometimes see this exhaustion get misconstrued as lack

of attention to detail on the CEO's part. But, again, it's not the CEO's job to be deep in the details. That's the job of the team. It's the *visibility*, not execution, of those details that CEOs actually need—a way for them, and everyone else on the team, to instantly be able to keep track of what's going on. A way for them to trust that things are on track without having to constantly zoom in and check for themselves. Essentially, what's needed is a system that allows teams to run the details themselves, and everyone to stay on the same page.

There are certain fundamental habits that make a team run fast, smooth, and consistently on track. Once they've mastered these fundamentals, teams don't need constant check-ins from the CEO; they don't need endless meetings to "get on the same page." I've had the privilege of being under the hood of so many companies that I earned a fluency in the fundamentals that make the machine run smoothly. I've worked with change agents for years, and I've seen what works and doesn't work.

The biggest takeaway from all the companies I've worked with is this: The teams that focus on and master the fundamentals are the teams that win.

As Bruce Lee once famously said: "I fear not the man who has practiced 10,000 kicks once, but I fear the man who has practiced one kick 10,000 times."

These fundamentals aren't *difficult*. They're just unknown to most companies. Or they're known by some individuals on the team, but the team doesn't have a system to reinforce the fundamentals and practice them over and over until they become muscle memory.

That's what I made Peak OS to do.

There are a lot of business operating systems out there, but there aren't any that deeply understand the unique challenges of VC-backed companies. As I developed Peak over the years and applied it to more and more businesses, it was reinforced to me over and over that VC-backed companies are in a class all their own. And Peak was custom-built to meet those companies where they are, then stay with them from pre-seed to exit. I've worked with companies from their first investment to their last investment; sometimes, I've even worked with the company that acquires them. This system is your guide throughout the entire journey—not just planning, but execution and operation as well. It allows you to quickly scope in and out from the smallest details to the big picture, and provides ultimate transparency to everyone involved (including your investors).

Building something revolutionary with no blueprint and no guarantee of success takes a special level of confidence and belief. As a VC-backed CEO, you've got that.

Now it's time to build the team that will successfully realize the vision you've sold to your investors, clients, employees, and the market.

This book will teach you how to master the core habits and

tools that will power that team.

HABITS > BEHAVIORS > RESULTS

One of the greatest lessons I've learned in my twenty years of working with VC-backed tech teams is that basically every myth associated with "tech people" is false.

The "lone genius"—nope, every Steve Jobs needs a Tim Cook. Focusing on innovation over everything else—that's a recipe for spinning in circles and never shipping a customer-ready product. I've seen it all at the many companies I've worked with in my career, and I've seen how many characteristics of VC-backed companies end up being speedbumps killing their velocity. And more often than not, there's a distinct tendency to ignore the human factor in the work—to try to systematize everything down to formulas of efficiency and productivity.

The human factor is what will take your company from struggling to reach targets to sailing toward a *very* lucrative exit. Ignore it at your own peril.

Another myth I hear a lot is what I call the "growth mode fallacy". "Of course it's chaotic; we're in growth mode! It *should* be chaotic!" Sound familiar?

This way of thinking is just plain wrong. Chaos is not a virtue. Organized teams win.

You can always spot an unstoppable team by their behaviors. In the hundreds of teams I've coached, I've seen a specific set of behaviors that *always* indicates a winning team—and without these behaviors, your team is likely to fall behind or get stuck.

- **Alignment**: Getting everyone on the same page about Why, Where, When, What, How, and most importantly, Who. Everyone needs to be moving in the same direction, or functionally, you're standing still.

- **Symbiosis**: Creating an environment of trust, respect, and unity. Without symbiosis, you'll notice silos forming and team members working independently from each other—sometimes even at odds without realizing it.

- **Communication**: What brings teams together and keeps them together. Poor communication absolutely kills morale and motivation, and along with them, your company's goals.

- **Empowerment**: Successful teams empower their members, providing autonomy and support for decision-making and ownership of work. When people have autonomy, they are more engaged, more creative, and more productive.

- **Learning**: A team that learns from itself is a team that constantly moves forward. We'll build the learning habit on both the individual and team levels.

I've divided this book into five parts, each covering one of these key behaviors and the specific ways the habits in Peak OS create and reinforce each one. This will also make it easy for you to flip to the behaviors you notice your team is weakest in—or that you've measured weakness in, with the Peak Teams Assessment. (If you want to check this out now, head to the Conclusion, where you'll find a link to take the assessment.)

A lot of the specific habits you're about to read about may be familiar to you. I've learned from the best in developing Peak; some of what you'll learn in this book is wisdom pulled together from sources you'll probably recognize.

The difference with Peak is that it works specifically for *you*, the venture-backed company. It works with all the energy, excitement, and speed that a tech startup brings to the table. Where you might have felt in the past that trying to apply regular habits to your team was like trying to fit a square peg in a round hole, Peak was created specifically for you and the people you lead. The habits you'll learn build the core behaviors that generate consistent top-level results.

Charles Duhigg, in his classic *The Power of Habit*, writes: "Champions don't do extraordinary things. They do ordinary things, but they do them without thinking, too fast for the other team to react. They follow the habits they've learned." That's what you're aiming for—habits so ingrained in your team that success happens without them having to think about it.

As you're reading, you may find yourself thinking, "This seems like extra work." Here's the good news: it's not. If anything, Peak simplifies your team's workload and gives you your time back. You'll learn easy ways for you to integrate Peak into your team's existing workflows. And, as your team starts down the Peak path, the wins they'll experience together will get them more and more excited to keep going. In the end, it will actually be *less* work, for *more* wins.

Peak has helped hundreds of companies just like yours accelerate to success. You'll read stories in each chapter that are mashups I've created of the many companies I've worked with (don't worry, Peak CEOs, all identifying details have been carefully removed!).

You'll also read real-world interviews with several Peak Teams CEOs throughout the book. Take their stories as an indication of what it will be like to take this journey with your own team.

THE PATH IS THE GOAL

Building the core habits that will empower your team and sky-rocket your company is a choice.

You can choose to continue the way you've been operating—with you, the CEO, trudging along exhausted, carrying the heaviest load on your own shoulders up the mountain.

But take it from me: it's no fun. And business is supposed to be fun! You're building something innovative and extraordinary, and your success can literally change the world. Wouldn't it be great if you actually got to enjoy yourself on the path?

You can. It's as simple as implementing the system in this book.

PART 1

TEAMS THAT WIN

ONE

MASTERING THE FUNDAMENTALS

"Habits are the invisible architecture of daily life."
–CHARLES DUHIGG

N 2022, OVER HALF A TRILLION VENTURE CAPITAL DOL-lars were invested in companies around the globe. The US is where a majority of those companies were located, with $241 billion going to US-based companies. Amazingly, this is actually a *decrease* from the peak of the recent VC gold rush in 2020 and 2021—and there's still a strong tailwind propelling money into companies at all stages. This appetite of investors will never go away. It may ebb and flow, but it will always be there as a strong demand. There will always be money to be raised.

And yet, despite all that cash flowing into VC-backed companies, twenty-five to thirty percent of them will fail. One in five fail by the end of their first year; only thirty percent will survive more than ten years.

That's an incredible amount of money that just disappears into the ether, despite the pressure placed on CEO Founders to produce a return. Any founder will immediately speak to the stress involved in running a VC-backed company, no matter if it's pre-seed or in Series D—they're putting everything they have into making the business work. But at the end of the day, about a third of them won't succeed. Seems like a bleak picture, doesn't it?

Here's the silver lining: if you can make it to a Series C, your chances of failure plummet. Pre-seed failure rates are around sixty percent; Series B failures are about thirty-five percent; but make it to Series C, and the failure rate goes to *one percent*. That's right. One. You're ninety-nine percent likely to make it if you can survive to that point.

But that's *still* not even the definition of success. Just making it through Series C doesn't mean you'll ever return money to your investors—which is the whole point of their investment. In fact, according to a Harvard study, 75 percent of venture-backed companies never return so much as a dime—and as many as 40 percent of those companies end up liquidating assets, their investors out of luck.

There are a lot of reasons companies fail. They get mismanaged, they get out-competed, they can't make the margins work—those are some common reasons. And if you're a founder, you're probably thinking about avoiding those every single day.

But what are the reasons companies *succeed*?

Is there a pattern that can be found, a secret sauce that separates the winners from the losers? Is there a blueprint that could show you the exact playbook that led one company to a high-dollar exit, and the next company to crash and burn?

After twenty years of working with companies at all stages, I can tell you that the answer to that is *yes*.

It's probably not what you think. It's not a particular product, funding amount, or even the mix of characteristics of the CEO Founder. Those things obviously matter, but they're not the secret sauce.

The difference between companies that succeed and companies that fail is their teams. Not the exact people on the team, although that's a piece of it. Not the work the teams are doing, although obviously that makes a difference, too.

Winning teams are differentiated by *how* they work, together and individually. How does the team operate on a daily basis? What is their culture? What are their core behaviors?

In this chapter, we're going to dive into the five core behaviors that your team absolutely *must* master if you want your company to not only survive, but thrive. We're going to investigate why these behaviors aren't innate to teams, and why building these behaviors is active, not passive. And finally, we're going to show that an unstoppable team has a system that reinforces key habits that build these behaviors, making the fundamentals part of every single thing they do, day in and day out, as the company climbs toward success.

THE WAY PEOPLE DO THINGS

Assembling a team of diverse talent, skill, and professional experience is a huge driver of success; you already know this. An echo chamber where everyone agrees will move forward a lot more slowly. This is because, when everyone thinks the same way, from the same base of past experience, far fewer ideas are brought to the table. As a founder, you've likely already taken care to bring together a wide array of viewpoints, talents, and skillsets—and even mindsets.

A natural side effect of bringing together skilled, successful experts, though, is that those people confuse "the way *we should do this*" with "the way *I've always done it*." Your CMO is bringing with them a totally different way of operating than your CTO, and if they've both experienced past success—which is likely, if they got hired—then they're going to want to default to their own way of doing things, because they've had positive feedback and results from doing it that way, or it's simply the only way they've ever done it.

Pretty soon, you're running a team that is actually a bunch of autonomous, disconnected routines running in their own grooves, like a machine that's Frankensteined together from a motley assortment of random tech.

And you don't want to kill the autonomy of your individual team members, or flatten the diversity that propels you forward, by making everyone do things the same way. This is why a lot of operating systems out there ultimately don't work; they try to over-manage a company's behaviors, and leave no space for the individual brilliance that is the reason you brought people into the team in the first place.

I've been under the hood of so many companies that I've had a front row seat to what works and what doesn't. I've been able to notice, test, and systematize the habits that stand out as true success drivers. That's what drove me to write this book; I've seen so many companies struggle not just with knowing they need a system to practice great team behaviors, but knowing exactly which behaviors are the ones that create results.

WINNING TEAM BEHAVIORS

Back (*way* back) in the year 2000, I was Chief of Staff to the CEO of a company called Gearworks, which was one of the first companies working on handheld mobile technology. We were developing a SaaS product for the very first generation of the Palm Pilot (remember those?). Think smartphone apps, before smartphones were a thing.

The team I was working with was filled with brilliant people working at the bleeding edge of the market. The company's CEO, Keith, was equally brilliant, and an especially powerful visionary and communicator. He could raise capital like no one I'd encountered up until that point in my career, and he had an incredible eye for talent. Thanks to his genius in picking the right people for the right roles, I was lucky enough to be working with one of the smartest groups of people I'd ever met.

Even with all that potential, though, we weren't truly a *team* until Bobby Crumpton came on board.

Bobby was hired as the CRO, and from his first day, I knew he was going to be the glue that really pulled the team together and got us working at our peak. This came as no surprise, either, because Bobby's background was in college sports; he'd been a West Point athlete and a professional coach. His experience on the field easily translated to the world of business. Bobby understood the power and value of an unstoppable team. He knew it was the only way to achieve the level of results the company needed, in a market where there was absolutely no roadmap for success. But more than that, he felt that being part of a well-operating team was so satisfying that he just didn't want to do it any other way. I believe that if he hadn't felt empowered to create a real team, he would have walked away from the role entirely.

Thanks to his coaching background, Bobby had an incredible fluency in what makes a team not just good, but *great*. And from day one, he was determined to make that happen at Gearworks.

It wasn't until Bobby started facilitating better collaboration that I realized the team had even been lacking in collaboration skills. Bobby taught us how to truly listen to each other and give everyone's ideas fair play. Allowing everyone to be part of the planning and decision-making for the business brought us together in a shared confidence. Everyone felt like they had a voice, and Bobby's confidence in all of us increased our trust in each other.

Bobby's true superpower was that he made everyone feel important. And in a team where everyone feels important, there's a heightened feeling of shared purpose that propels work forward far faster and farther than it would have gotten otherwise.

I came away from that experience understanding for the first time that unity and togetherness aren't characteristics that automatically exist within a team. Unity has to be created with action, and it has to be maintained with intention. It's actually not difficult if you give it the attention it deserves—you'd be surprised at how much teams *want* to be unified and act with shared purpose.

That experience was one of many over the following twenty years of working with companies at all stages—from pre-seed to exit—that showed me the behaviors that stood out in the most successful teams. There are five core team behaviors that are foundational to the success of a VC-backed company. Without these five behaviors deeply ingrained and constantly reinforced, results won't happen. Put another way, there are a lot of important behaviors to build, but these are the five deal-breakers your team needs to build and *master* in order to win:

1. Alignment
2. Symbiosis
3. Communication
4. Empowerment
5. Learning

ALIGNMENT

Alignment is about *agreement*—agreeing on the where and when, the what and how, the why and who. The team must first agree on where you're going before you can define what you have to do to get there. From alignment you bring about focus; from focus, accountability; and from accountability, you get results.

You know a team has mastered alignment when they are all in *agreement* on these basic questions:

1. **Why** are we doing this?
2. **Where** are we going?
3. **When** will we get there?
4. **What** do we need to do to get there?
5. **How** will we do it?
6. **Who** are we, and who do we need on the team to succeed?

The core characteristic of alignment is that the team has discussed these questions and *is in agreement on them.* You can't assume they are; you'd be surprised at how many teams think they're in alignment, but aren't.

A team in alignment will all have the same answers when you ask them those questions, and their understanding of those answers will guide all the hundreds of micro-decisions they make each day as they do their work. With alignment, even a large team—and an organization made up of several large teams—can all move in the same direction without scattering or getting distracted.

SYMBIOSIS

Symbiosis is when everyone is working together in unity, thriving in an environment of trust and respect. Everyone is trusted to execute their unique role and achieve their agreed-upon results; everyone trusts their teammates to have their back and not let the team down. And as a thriving team, everyone is driving toward a shared purpose and goals that have been clearly defined and communicated. The team works together collectively to successfully achieve the mission and vision of the organization. The attitude is one of abundance; the rising tide lifts all boats, and by doing what's best for the company, everyone wins.

Could I have called this habit "synergy"? Sure. But that word has been overused to death, and it also doesn't connote the living, breathing feeling of a symbiotic relationship. Symbiosis is about *people*, and it can't be manufactured.

COMMUNICATION

Communication is what brings teams together and keeps teams together.

You can immediately tell when a team isn't practicing the habit of communication. Tasks take longer to complete, problems are discussed (often endlessly) but never truly solved, and priorities sit on the back burner while time is wasted. People aren't clear on their roles and responsibilities, so they're not working efficiently or cooperatively, and trust is eroded.

Whereas, in a team where the habit of communication has been mastered, everyone has the opportunity to speak and be heard. And even when someone's ideas aren't adopted as the solution the team pursues, that person still feels recognized, and instead of "agreeing to disagree", they'll "disagree and still commit" to the direction the team has decided on. People are clear on the mission and objectives the team is working toward, and they're committed and accountable to their roles and responsibilities. Trust throughout the organization is so strong you can practically feel it in the air. Things get *done*.

EMPOWERMENT

Empowerment is the habit that is going to create the most freedom for you, the CEO, and your team. This is the one that, more than any other, gets you out of the stress spiral.

Empowered team members are more likely to take risks, generate new ideas, and think outside the box. When team members feel empowered, they have a sense of ownership over their work and are more likely to be engaged and motivated to succeed. Thanks to practicing the habits of communication and alignment, team members are crystal clear on their roles; and with clarity of roles, team members have the freedom to make decisions and take action without constantly seeking approval from their leaders.

In *Trillion Dollar Coach*, the authors, Eric Schmidt, Jonathan Rosenberg, and Alan Eagle, write about the leadership practices of Bill Campbell, legendary Silicon Valley coach and business executive. Empowering team members with autonomy was one of the main ways Campbell drove trust in organizations.

> "Bill's genius was in recognizing the universal applicability of respect in every situation, at every level of an organization. He understood that when people feel valued, they perform at the top of their game and enjoy doing it."

When people feel empowered, they feel *respected*. And when people feel respected, their motivation and performance peak.

LEARNING

In his bestseller *Drive*, Daniel H. Pink emphasizes the importance of mastery and learning.

> "The desire to do something because you find it deeply satisfying and personally challenging inspires the highest levels of creativity, whether it's in the arts, sciences, or business."

A team that practices learning as a habit will be agile and nimble at problem-solving, creative and organized in the process of discovery, and responsive to change, not resistant. Outside talent can immediately spot an environment where learning is fostered via those signals of growth and productivity, and they'll be attracted to the company as a place where they can level up.

SYSTEMATIZE TEAM HABITS

So, how do you ensure that these behaviors are practiced so consistently and built so strongly that your team lives and breathes them? How do you ensure that Alignment, Symbiosis, Communication, Empowerment, and Learning are reinforced day in and day out without your team even being asked to pay attention to them?

This is where Peak comes into play, and will be the course we chart through the rest of this book.

I designed Peak to build the core habits your team needs to operate at their best without feeling like they're constrained or micromanaged. Peak isn't extra work; it's the *way* you work.

Most importantly, it's a living, breathing system that allows your organization to operate as the fast-moving, constantly changing, growth-oriented organism it needs to be to innovate and compete. It's flexible; you don't have to wait until conditions in your company bring you to a good "starting point".

You don't have to wait until it's "planning time" at the start of the year.

Start where you are. Start right now.

Peak works because it's a repeating cycle of *everything* you need to do to facilitate the core Team Habits and keep your team driving toward your North Star—the company's mission, what you're all trying to accomplish.

The best part is that it's easy. It truly is.

That's not to say it's *simple*; there's a lot you're going to learn over the next several chapters, and I don't recommend trying to roll out the entire system all at once. That's the beauty of Peak; you can introduce elements of the system to your team at *their* pace, meeting them where they are. You don't have to throw out what you've already been doing. On the contrary, the unique perspective you have based on how far your company has already come will inform how you adopt this system and complement it, not conflict with it.

Peak isn't something you'll do once and forget about. It will stay with your company from pre-seed to exit. It will keep your teams aligned, motivated, and driving forward, with a structure that takes the load off of "figuring out what to do". And for you, as the leader, that stress spiral will melt away. You'll have all the visibility into the details you need, and you'll trust that your team is empowered to own them.

Building winning behaviors is powerful. As I said in the

Introduction, though, it's a choice. You and your team have to *choose* to live this system in order to reinforce the core behaviors that are the difference between success and failure. You have to *choose* to be in the tiny percentage of companies that will succeed. And you have to be active in reinforcing that choice, day in and day out.

The way your team does anything is the way they do everything, and my aim with this book is to empower your team to become a Peak Team. With Peak, you have the guidebook to craft and evolve your team's behavior to ensure you'll all win together.

TWO

A SYSTEM OF HABITS

"Talent wins games, but teamwork
and intelligence win championships."
—MICHAEL JORDAN

TAKING A CASUAL DAY HIKE DOESN'T REQUIRE A TON OF upfront planning. You gather some friends (or your dog), you find a nice trail nearby, and you just start walking—no particular destination in mind. You're there to unwind in nature and get your blood pumping, have fun, and see all the interesting landmarks along the way. There's no real end goal. Sometimes you don't even bring along extra water; you can always turn back to your car parked at the trailhead when you feel tired or thirsty.

Now contrast that vibe with an *expedition*, which may take days, weeks, or even months. The first major difference is that there's a goal: you're aiming to make it to a summit or a particular destination, and that's the whole point of being there in the first place. The second major difference is that you have to nail down your strategy, tactics, and supplies ahead of time, or you won't make it to the top. There's no turning back to the car when you get thirsty. If you pick the wrong people to go on your expedition team, you'll be held back. Every item in your rucksack has to be carefully considered for its weight-to-usefulness ratio. You have to continually check in with your compass and GPS to make sure you're still on the right path and haven't accidentally stumbled onto a longer or rockier route. In short, the expedition is only as good as the planning you put into it, the continual adherence to that plan, and careful course-correction if you find that something isn't working.

With the stakes so incredibly high in a venture-backed company, it would make sense for its leadership team to treat the business like an expedition rather than a day hike. In my experience with CEOs, not one of them would disagree with that.

But in reality, despite perhaps starting out with an expedition plan, many, many companies unravel from a coordinated expedition into a series of day hikes, one after another. In an expedition lasting a year, you could climb all of the tallest peaks in the world. But 365 day hikes in a row? You'll just be worn out and wondering why you're even doing it in the first place.

Peak turns those constant day hikes into a coordinated expedition. Your team knows how to climb; they've made it to the peak where the company currently sits, and they've proven that they have what it takes. What your team needs now is a system to accelerate them into the next stage of your journey. This system will align everyone in the right direction, and will build and reinforce the core habits that maximize their time, capital, and energy—leading all of you to finish together on top of the summit.

In this chapter, you'll learn a broad overview of the entire Peak Operating System. Like I mentioned in Chapter One, this system is the opposite of the "simple, not easy" saying; it's *not* simple, but once you get rolling, it *is* easy.

The key takeaway I want you to remember is that you don't have to "nail" the system "start to finish", because the start is right where you are now. Don't overcomplicate things; just start where you are with the tools your team can confidently wrap its arms around. As you build into implementing the entire system, the self-reinforcing nature of the habits and tools will make it easier and more instinctive week after week. Don't try to run before you've mastered walking; as they say in the Navy SEALs, "Slow is smooth, smooth is fast."

With that in mind, this chapter serves as a reference for you to flip back to while you make your way through the system in the chapters to come. I recommend bookmarking this chapter so you always have it on hand as you're learning.

PEAK OS ACCESS FOR PEAK TEAMS

When you get started with Peak, you'll have this book as a reference, and you'll be guided for at least your first year—ideally two years—by your Peak Coach (throughout this book, you'll see me play the role of Coach in the stories that walk you through Peak). You can reach out to Collective Genius at any time to get started with your Peak Coach.

In addition, all Peak Teams subscribe to Peak OS Access, an online resource and knowledge base that acts as your go-to reference for the system. You'll find digital tools there like the Peak Team Dashboard (which you'll learn about soon) and all the instructions needed to get started now. You can also use Peak OS Access to self-implement Peak right away by teaching a Guide you select in your company. Peak OS Access is available immediately, even before you plan your Launch Session, and is a great resource to take advantage of.

Check it out: *collective-genius.com/peak-os-access*.

START WITH ALIGNMENT

When climbing a mountain, Base Camp is the staging area for the expedition. Base Camp is also where climbers rest and acclimatize to the higher altitude. If you've been feeling the wear and tear of the grind your team has been in, Base Camp is a key moment to relax and come together as a team. It's an important point of reflection before you look to embark on the next climb.

Base Camp is where the specific route to the next peak is planned. Here's how we plan that route in Peak Teams:

- **Mission Statement**: This is your company's North Star, the Why behind what your team is doing. It's critical for the team to understand their Why if they're going to believe in the expedition and go all in.

- **Three Year Vision** (3YV): Your North Star is way off in the distance, so we start by planning a route to an achievable destination, which for VC-backed companies is three years out. I've found this to be the magic number for both early and late stage companies. We think of the 3YV as three mountain peaks away from Base Camp. It's the peak where you and your team will be standing in three years' time. The Three Year Vision provides alignment to the team and gives them a tangible understanding where they are going and when they will be there; it's a direction and time frame for the expedition.

- **One Year Plan** (1YP): You've established a destination three peaks away from Base Camp, so the next step is to plan the route to the top of the peak right in front of you. Remember, you're going to start where you are. It's okay if you're in the middle of the year; your first 1YP will get you to the end of the year you're in. The peak of this 1YP is what your team agrees is their destination and definition of success by the end of the year.

MISSION STATEMENT

Simon Sinek, in his groundbreaking book *Start With Why*, writes: "All organizations start with *why*, but only the great ones keep their *why* clear year after year."

One of the most common challenges I see unfold in VC-backed companies is a failure to re-align to the company's Why after it's originally set by the founders. I find that interesting, because the Why is often the most exciting part! It's what got founders, early investors, and the first team members fired up in the first place. It's the whole purpose behind every day of work the company accomplishes. Getting everyone aware and clear on the mission upfront is a stabilizing and inspiring moment that sets the tone for the planning to come.

When I start guiding companies through Peak, we always spend part of the Launch session—the very first Planning session, starting wherever your team is right now—aligning on the mission statement of the company and *why* they're on this expedition together. I often see that even in teams who have worked together for years, the definition of this Why isn't always clear and agreed-upon. Getting aligned on what the entire team is there for is the fuel that keeps their fire stoked throughout the climb. As Sinek puts it:

> There are only two ways to influence human behavior: you can manipulate it or you can inspire it.
>
> Very few people or companies can clearly articulate *why* they do *what* they do. By *why* I mean your purpose, cause or belief—*why* does your company exist? *Why* do you get out of bed every morning? And *why* should anyone care?
>
> People don't buy *what* you do, they buy *why* you do it.
>
> We are drawn to leaders and organizations that are good at communicating what they believe. Their ability to make us feel like we belong, to make us feel special, safe and not alone is part of what gives them the ability to inspire us.
>
> Happy employees ensure happy customers. And happy customers ensure happy shareholders—in that order.

Your team's North Star isn't an earthly location you're going to eventually stand on. It's up in the sky as a guiding light, providing you the direction to orient to no matter where you are on the expedition. It provides the team with inspiration and calls them to movement.

It's also possible that the North Star may need to be re-examined from time to time. This is typically indicated when the team has started to fragment in alignment. It's entirely possible that the team's direction has changed or lost focus, and they need to align to a new mission statement. You'll circle back on this Why and ensure the team's agreement at key points throughout the expedition.

THREE YEAR VISION

Climbers call the series of peaks that leads them to their summit the Haute Route (high route) or Ridge Route. We create your team's Ridge Route by pinpointing the spot three peaks out and the route of peaks it will take to get there.

Sitting in Base Camp, it's important for the team to understand not only where they're going, but also when they intend to arrive there. By doing so, everyone will start climbing together in the same direction. The 3YV also provides context for everyone on the team on the *duration* and *pace* of travel, which is what allows you to accurately allocate resources. That last point is incredibly important in the fast-paced environment of a VC-backed company; it's common for teams to completely overestimate their capacity and underestimate the time and resources it will take to get to a certain goal.

The benefit of the entire team creating the 3YV together is tremendous. It allows the whole team ownership over the crucial high-level aspects of the Why and Where of their mission. It also aligns everyone on a vision and message that can be clearly communicated—especially to the business's many stakeholders, including investors and the Board. Finally, it takes the guesswork out of hiring; with the increased clarity and alignment the 3YV creates on everyone's roles, it functionally acts as a hiring roadmap. It also serves as a talent magnet, as high-quality candidates are going to be far more likely to join a team that is unified and energized by a clearly communicated direction. They're inspired to want to join that journey.

ONE YEAR PLAN

The One Year Plan (1YP) is a further drilling down into details, shortening the map of the team's work to the time period that stretches up until the next Annual Session. It's important to remember the key takeaway about Peak, which I'll be repeating many more times throughout this book: *don't wait until the start of the year.* Start where you are. Start right now. Does "right now" happen to be January? Incredible, then you're conveniently kicking off with what will become your Annual Session. Is right now more like August? Also incredible: your team's launch session covers only the few months left until the end of the year, which is going to make it feel even more achievable.

The 1YP can also be thought of as the tactical details of a strategy based on vision. Peak is such an effective guide alongside your team on its journey because it guides you to regularly map and operate on the company's vision, its strategy, and its tactics. And as the CEO, you'll be freed up from needing to be constantly directing in all three of those levels at all times.

This is a challenge I hear the CEOs I work with speak about frequently: the need to remind their teams where they're headed and how they're supposed to be getting there. Teams lack an easy reference and reinforcement of their direction and objectives.

With a 1YP, the team will be able to see a clear line of waypoints leading their climb up to the peak of the first mountain— the end of the current year. The clarity provided by the 1YP is a massive driver of individual accountability at the team level, and team accountability at the company level. It also saves the CEO that exhaustion I spoke about earlier, from constantly zooming in and out from big vision to small detail. Team members stay ultra-clear on where they're going and what they're supposed to be doing, so the need to zoom in and remind them disappears. It's no longer a guess what people are working on, or how their role is contributing to the overall climb up the mountain. The 1YP is a clear map of exactly where each hiker is aiming and what they need to do to get there.

FINDING SYMBIOSIS

On a day hike, there's not much need to measure what you're doing, how far you've gone, your pace, or your elevation. You don't have a larger goal you're trying to hit; you're just out to have a good time and then go back to the comfort of your car.

But setting out on an expedition without a way to measure your climb could literally mean the difference between life and death.

Serious climbers with a goal in mind constantly measure their speed, elevation, the amount of food and water they have left, and health markers to make sure their bodies are handling the demand—not to mention GPS so they know they're still on the trail in the first place.

Your team is no different. They need regular milestones to act as a measurement of their journey, give them confidence in their progress, and allow them to catch themselves early if they're moving off-course. Peak will help your team chart KPIs and OKRs that keep them moving in the same direction smoothly.

KPIs

I've seen many companies procrastinate in setting these up. Or they'll share some basic top-level financial metrics with the board, but fail to create and track real KPIs internally with their teams.

That's skipping over the fundamentals. KPIs are fundamentals that need to be practiced and mastered. I often tell teams that with KPIs, we're *measuring the business to learn the business*. And the insights gained are going to make it easier for all of them to get better at what they do.

Setting KPIs as a team helps everyone gain ownership of the way their work is being measured. You also benefit from everyone seeing how their individual contribution fits into the overall picture. KPIs originate at the leadership level, and each one breaks down into several more sub-metrics at the team level. Everyone can see how the KPIs they're responsible for contribute to the success of the climb, from each individual on the team all the way up to the CEO. Start small, then measure, learn, master, and eventually conquer your market.

OKRS

Just as a team of mountain climbers define clear goals (reaching the next peak) and measurable steps (maintaining pace, checking equipment) to reach their summit, a venture-backed team uses Objectives and Key Results (OKRs) to scale operations.

Let's dive first into a breakdown of the term. Objectives and Key Results are different things, and together they create a map of work that drives the team forward toward completing their 1YP and driving toward their 3YV.

An Objective is a What. "We're trying to make it to X point on our one-year plan; *what* do we need to do to get there?"

A Key Result is a How. "*How* will we achieve that objective, and how will we measure it?"

Let's say the objective is a successful product launch; the key results may be a well-defined one-month product roadmap from Product, delivering to specific epics from Engineering, implementing a marketing launch from Marketing, and a go-to-market strategy from Sales.

OKRs allow a team to build their capabilities through focused, measured, and cross-functional initiatives across all key departments. With OKRs, the team is able to practice focus and prioritization on a regular cadence so that it becomes intuitive and deeply ingrained into their natural workflows. And by defining how the objective will be accomplished and measured together as a team, symbiosis is created, which leads to results.

OKRs are defined every 90 days, and should always be anchored in the objectives defined by the 1YP and 3YV. The OKRs your team defines and iterates on each quarter should form a clear series of waypoints up the side of the mountain towards the peak.

EFFECTIVE COMMUNICATION

One of the most common gripes I hear from teams at all kinds of companies is that there are too many meetings on the calendar. This tends to happen when no *system* for effective meetings exists, and people simply toss meetings on the calendar whenever they need to hash something out. It's a sign of ineffective communication, and turning that communication *effective* requires some basic guardrails.

With Peak, the concept of "meeting for meeting's sake" is thrown out. The system's base unit of communication is the Weekly Camp Meeting, or "Camp".

Week over week, the team will follow a clearly defined meeting structure in the Weekly Camp Meeting. The Weekly Camp Meeting is where everything comes together and stays together. It is a pivotal meeting, a cadence that allows the teams to regularly review their OKRs and KPIs, have focused conversations, define and solve problems, and keep the team moving forward with action.

At the Weekly Camp Meeting, the team comes together after a week of focused climbing. They review waypoints, discuss open topics and issues, and plan any changes for the coming week. Then they get back to the climb with nothing distracting them from the next week's worth of trail winding ahead of them up the next section of the mountain.

TRIAGE

I've seen so many companies fall victim to endlessly talking about their problems instead of actually solving them. It feels like the team is communicating, because the same issues keep being brought up meeting after meeting and there's endless discussion; but no solution is ever reached, and the conversation just keeps spinning like a hamster wheel.

Peak uses a key tool called Triage to build great communication in your team. Triage is a clearinghouse for communication, a way to categorize, prioritize, and organize issues that need to be discussed. In each Weekly Camp Meeting, Triage provides a framework and agenda for tackling issues together as a team. It's the tool that keeps the team agile in a fast changing environment, and teaches them to not only discuss issues, but actually *solve them*. They walk out of the meeting feeling relieved, confident, and pumped that they actually wiped out the topics on their list and gained momentum.

Keeping issues consolidated and systematically worked within the Triage tool prevents chaos—and cuts down on the reactivity that leads to random, ineffective meetings thrown on the calendar. We'll take a deeper look at the Triage tool and how iteration is accomplished at each cadence in the coming chapters.

AN EMPOWERED ORGANIZATION

Empowerment arises from each member of the team having a clear understanding of their unique contribution to the entire expedition.

ROLES AND RESPONSIBILITIES

Peak helps your team build empowerment by breaking down clearly each person's Role and Responsibilities in the context of the entire team's goal, and the objectives of the whole organization.

How often do you experience team members going to the CEO constantly to ask for smaller decisions that should be owned by team members—or worse, staying frozen in place? This is a result of a lack of clarity in who owns decisions. You may also have experienced two team members battling it out or stepping on each other's toes because it's not clear who owns what. And how many times have you noticed that somehow, there always seems to be gaps in the skills and responsibilities you need to accomplish your mission?

Peak ensures that each team member clearly understands both their own ownership and their teammates'—and the empowerment they have to fully own their results.

TALENT MAPPING

In the classic *Good to Great*, Jim Collins writes:

The executives who ignited the transformations from good to great did not first figure out where to drive the bus and then get people to take it there. No, they first got the right people on the bus (and the wrong people off the bus) and then figured out where to drive it. They said, in essence, "Look, I don't really know where we should take this bus. But I know this much: If we get the right people on the bus, the right people in the right seats, and the wrong people off the bus, then we'll figure out how to take it someplace great."

Talent Mapping is a key tool that will help you figure out not only who the right people on the bus are, but the exact seats the bus needs to get to its destination fastest.

You'll start by mapping out the key functional areas that report to the CEO, and outline roles, responsibilities, and twelve-month objectives. You'll also map the ideal skills and experiences needed for each role. Then, align your current leadership team with these functional roles, identifying any mismatches in skills, values, or motivation. Pinpoint gaps and decide whether to upskill current leaders or recruit new ones. The most important thing to identify is each team member's alignment with the company's core values and genuine motivation for their role—a mismatch on either likely means they're the wrong person, in the wrong seat, or both.

BUILD A LEARNING TEAM

Teams learn by repetition. We accomplish this in Peak in two main ways:

1. **Team Surveys:** Reviewing how the team is doing in regular surveys that ask about the fundamentals. In looking at where they've come from and analyzing where they currently stand, teams build the learning muscle by constantly learning from the past.

2. **Cadence:** This predictable rhythm of teamwork creates an environment that instills learning behaviors and reinforces the habits of repetition and mastery.

TEAM SURVEYS

Reviewing where you've come from with Team Surveys is crucial to understanding where you are, and where the starting point of your next climb is. It's a big difference between Peak and other systems that jump right into vision and planning; even when your team has their Launch Session, you'll start team surveys that everyone completes before gathering.

The insights you'll gain from these surveys range from validating—enjoying the view of the success you've achieved so far—to enlightening, when you realize there are key aspects of your expedition the team is *not* aligned on, or that there are areas of the mission still unclear to members of the team. I've seen CEOs who are surprised by the results of their first Peak Teams Survey. But that's okay; once the misalignment is out in the open, Peak is what will get your team back on track.

CADENCE

After 90 days of the Weekly Camp Meeting, the team will gather for the Quarterly Session. The team reviews the previous quarter, checking in with waypoints and surveys, and also reviews the 1YP in its entirety and from their new vantage point 90 days higher on the mountain than they were when they made the plan. As necessary, they'll iterate, making course corrections. Then they realign to their waypoints, potentially planning new or adjusted KPIs, and creating new 90-day OKRs—the waypoints to the next base camp 90 days out.

They continue on these cadences—Weekly Camp Meetings and Quarterly Sessions every 90 days—until they reach the end of the year. At that point, they should be at or ahead of their 1YP.

This is where the final cadence comes in: the Annual Session. At the Annual, you'll review the entire past year with your team, celebrating wins and taking in lessons. Then you'll walk through the Roles and Responsibilities of each member of the team, cast a new Three Year Vision and One Year Plan, and map out your OKRs for Q1.

Again, you don't have to wait for the new year to start with your Launch Session. Start now.

GET THE FUNDAMENTALS, GET TO THE SUMMIT

With the incredibly fast pace of VC-backed companies, focusing on the fundamentals often falls by the wayside in favor of ever-shifting strategy and tactics. But the fundamentals are how your team members stay in sight of each other on the mountain, and how they trust each person to be accountable to their role and responsibilities. Without a mastery of the fundamentals, you might as well be trying to hike in a thick fog. Clarity comes from alignment, and without alignment, there can be no unity. You want your team not only aligned, but also *inspired* by your mission. You want them to be able to clearly communicate that mission to stakeholders, clients, and investors. You want your shared mission to effortlessly guide each micro decision and micro action taken minute after minute, hour after hour, throughout each workday.

The way to the peak is built on the smallest of habits. The goal of Peak is to integrate the habits we've walked through in this chapter into the team's daily, weekly, quarterly, and annual workflows so they're practicing the fundamentals without even thinking about it.

That's the true power of this system: your team will be naturally building the core habits of unstoppable companies without having to exert thought or action. It will just *happen*. You'll notice them getting leaner, stronger, and faster with each cadence that passes.

Habits build *winning behaviors* that unlock *results*.

Ready to start?

Turn to Part Two to begin your team's journey.

CASE STUDY: DATABOOK

I conducted this interview with Anand Shah,
CEO and Co-Founder of Databook

Starting a company always has its challenges, and they're magnified intensely when you've raised venture capital. So few businesses that start out actually progress to Series B. I remember when we raised our seed round in January 2020, every day felt like a battle for survival, leaving little time to structure or organize. Four years in, it was long past time for some semblance of order, which led us to introducing Peak into our operations.

It was essential for us to get everything out on the table, from our three-year vision to our quarterly plans. Establishing a vision was vital to our operation, and once we got that down on paper, the whole team got a clear idea of our objectives. However, not everything went as smoothly as we would have hoped. I remember mapping out our growth and realizing the unexpected need to significantly expand our customer success group. We managed to do it, but it was a huge wake-up call, reminding us of the importance of planning and connecting the dots ahead of time to avoid nasty surprises.

When diving into the realm of OKRs, the first thing that struck me was how much it felt like a personality test for the CEO. I've always been someone who thrives on structure and organization, but I've also come to realize that I can't track every detail. My strength lies in zooming in and out, moving quickly between the big picture and finer details, and especially focusing on the most pressing priorities.

Initially, we tried implementing organizational, team, and individual OKRs. But balancing all three became tough, so we decided to prioritize organizational and individual OKRs. This approach created a lot of clarity and bridged the gap between company-wide goals and individual responsibilities.

If you're not tracking key results effectively, they're of little use. In cases where we couldn't find a direct metric, we relied on proxies. And if even those weren't available, we opted not to measure, as it only added to our already hefty workload.

Implementing OKRs isn't just about buying software or tools. It demands a transformation of your organization—lasting changes in people, mindset, and systems.

When I look back, it's clear we've come a long way. Surviving, let alone thriving, in this space is no small feat, and having metrics and data to guide us made all the difference. The team has seen a ton of changes; many from our initial team have moved on, leading to new members adapting to our OKR approach. In essence, our journey has been about learning, adapting, and constantly seeking better ways to drive our vision forward.

If I were to advise a founder who is currently standing where I was three years ago, I'd stress the importance of coordination and organization. Not everyone is a fan of OKRs or tracking systems; some people find them restrictive and overbearing. This is why it's essential for the CEO to lead by example and drive the initiative. If it's just delegated with no clear endorsement from the top, it won't stick. The idea behind OKRs is for everyone to understand the business and learn from it. As a founder, you might need to push harder and be more assertive to ensure everyone stays on the same page.

PART 2

ALIGNMENT

THREE

WORKING HARD TO STAND STILL

"In any moment of decision, the best thing you can
do is the right thing, the next best thing is the wrong
thing, and the worst thing you can do is nothing."
—THEODORE ROOSEVELT

WHEN PEOPLE TALK ABOUT CHICAGO WINTERS, THEY
definitely don't oversell just how cold and windy it is. If
anything, they *undersell* it. I grew up in Minnesota, and
even I cringe at the thought of February in the Windy City.
Which is exactly where I found myself several years ago
when I held a Peak Teams session for a Series A FinTech team

I'd just started working with. It was a balmy minus-twenty degrees as I walked stiffly into an icy wind, the four blocks from my hotel in downtown Chicago to the company's offices having seemed like no big deal. Ten seconds in, my face hurt, and I regretted my decision. Some people say I've grown weak with all my years living in southern California—but I like to think of it as *experienced*.

I'd had dinner the previous evening with the company's CEO at the famous pizza joint Lou Malnati's. We met up to connect and discuss some last-minute team updates she had. There would be one new leadership team member joining the session from an acquisition they'd just made, and there were some other interesting team dynamics at play.

"I just want to prep you," she'd said, "things might be a little touchy at this session. Our Head of Sales and Head of Product are constantly at odds with each other. I'm hoping your time doesn't get wasted on another one of their battles."

This hadn't come as a surprise to me. I'd already met the entire team (minus the new team member) on our pre-session call, and had spent my four-hour flight from LA reviewing their Peak Team Survey. I had a good feel for where the team was currently at—which was pretty obviously out of alignment.

"I feel like we're all trying really hard to work together, but something is missing," the CEO had continued. "We all have the best of intentions and a lot of drive. But the details just keep getting lost from one team to the next. Some days I feel like we all understand what we're doing...then the next day I find another team going in a totally different direction."

Over a pepperoni deep dish, I had listened to the CEO pour out her frustrations, and then told her something that typically surprises a lot of CEOs and Founders: What she was describing was not just something I'd encountered before; it was actually quite common in VC-backed companies.

"This is not uncommon for many teams I meet for the first time," I'd said, and watched as relief washed across her features. "And it's truly not too difficult to get everyone aligned and get your team uplifted quickly if they're willing to lean in and trust the process. Do you think they're willing to do that?"

"Definitely," she'd said enthusiastically. "We all want to feel better and do better."

And now, after surviving the freezing stroll from my hotel and making my way into the company's conference room, I could see right away she was telling the truth. Everyone in the room had shown up with a great attitude.

Everyone but one person, that is. The Head of Product showed some signs of not being fully committed to the session.

He'd shown up unprepared, where everyone else had done their pre-session work and shown up ready to get things done. As the team started talking through issues, he struggled to take accountability for anything involving his own team. He was showing the signs of a lone wolf; he had his own agenda, which was different from the team's agenda. You've undoubtedly encountered these signs in people before: they can't hear others' ideas, they won't accept any other way than *their* way, and they refuse to follow through on any team decision that they don't agree with.

There was tension in the room centered around his energy. I knew that any progress made by the team in this session would have to involve a major change in his behavior and attitude, or he'd continue to be a drag on their efforts.

Over the next hour, I heard all kinds of frustrations from the team—and more signs of a lack of alignment.

The CEO and CFO shared that when prepping for a recent board meeting, they realized they each had two different end-of-year revenue goal numbers, and neither was the same as the number that had been shared with the board the previous month.

The Engineering team was not on track for a product launch Marketing was preparing.

Another co-founder had been spending his time building an international go-to-market strategy, but the CEO and Head of Sales hadn't planned on going international for another few years.

Story after story of enthusiastic progress forward by one team...in a different direction than everyone else was moving in. With the constant push and pull between functional areas of the business, they'd fallen behind on momentum. They were heads down in grind mode every day, but getting nowhere. They were frustrated and drained—drained of time, energy, *and* capital.

They were completely lacking in Alignment. And without this core team behavior, they weren't going to get anywhere close to their goals.

As the weather outside shifted to a light (for Chicago, at least) snowfall, I began to walk them through the tool that would get them aligned and then help them continuously build the alignment muscle over the quarters to come. It's where I always start with teams during their Launch Session: The Three Year Vision and One Year Plan.

I kicked off this part of the session with a Dandapani quote I love: "You wouldn't just get in your car and start driving. Why would you do that with your life or business?"

I saw a few heads nod slightly in agreement.

With this signal that they were on board, I had everyone pull up the Peak Team Surveys they'd completed as part of their prep work for the session (two to three weeks prior to the session, the team will get a few questions to work on with their teams, as well as the Peak Teams Survey). I always kick off any session with the team reviewing their surveys together. It helps for them to walk through it, talk through each question on the survey, and see with their own eyes where they're on track or misaligned. I think of it as unpacking their thoughts so we can really get some work done. (It also leads to some interesting moments as people call out things like, "What—someone gave Communication a *two*?!")

By walking through the survey together and making sure everyone has the opportunity to be heard, we're being proactive about alignment from the start—we're not leaving alignment to chance.

And, after walking through this team's surveys, some key things stood out.

"It sounds like we're aligned on our mission, would you all agree?" Nods from the team.

"However, it sounds like we may have less clarity or agreement on where we are going and what we may need to do to get there—correct?" More nods.

Up on the screen where I was delivering my deck, an image of three mountain peaks appeared.

"This peak represents where we will be three years from now. What will we have accomplished at this point?"

"Why three years?" This was from the Head of Product, of course. "That's way too far out. Most of us don't even know what we need to do *tomorrow*."

"What I've found with both early-stage and late-stage teams is that three years out is the sweet spot," I told him. "It's important to define where we want to go and define a tangible point in the future to draw our path there."

I could see that the room was all in. I'd given them a highly achievable goal; three years was a concrete time period and target they could picture, think into, and have a real discussion about.

"So, where do we want to be three years out?"

I asked them to pull out their prep work, which contained a series of questions I had them considering with their teams prior to the session.

They all pulled out the three year question and we wrote each of their answers to the question for their functional area on the whiteboard. As the minutes slipped away and the team got deeper and deeper into the discussion, I saw something I hadn't seen when I'd first walked into the room with them.

It was excitement. There was a huge renewal of energy. The tension simmering under the surface had abated—maybe temporarily, but even so, it was a welcome energy shift. Finally, here was something tangible that would point them all in the same direction.

By the end of the day, we had a Three Year Vision, a One Year Plan, and the upcoming quarter's objectives mapped out. "Wow," said the CEO, looking at the day's work, "I can't believe we were missing something so simple."

It's something I see all the time when teaching Peak OS— surprise at how what seem like the smallest, most obvious steps make the biggest difference.

Sometimes finding alignment really is just as simple as all agreeing where you want to go, and drawing a map to get there together.

FOUR

FROM ALIGNMENT TO FOCUS TO RESULTS

"Coming together is a beginning, staying together
is progress, and working together is success."
–HENRY FORD

H OW MANY TIMES IN YOUR LIFE—BOTH PERSONAL AND professional—have you been told to focus?

From the time we're kids in school and all through our careers, we're told that focus is the key to getting things done. Maybe you even have kids yourself now and can recall the last time you told them they need to focus; it was probably recent, right?

Now answer this question: were you ever *taught* how to focus?

If you were, shoot me an email and tell me where, because I've never seen a class on it. I certainly never took one. And I've noticed that throughout the professional landscape, the number one piece of advice given to business leaders is to do something none of us were ever actually taught to do.

As a leader within a VC-backed company, focus is the most important thing you can get your team to do. Getting everyone to narrow their view and stay on target within the often chaotic, innovation-rich, constantly evolving environment of your company is easier said than done. You now have even a bigger challenge: you need to get an entire team to focus on something that has never been done before. Sounds daunting, right?

I see a lot of leadership teams just believe that a lack of focus is "just part of the deal"—but it doesn't need to be.

Before your team can get focused, they have to get *aligned*. They need to agree on where they're going before they can decide what they'll do to get there, how they'll do those things, and even who they'll need with them on the journey.

It's a lot like setting out on a long expedition, all your gear strapped to your backs, everyone excited to climb—but no one knows what direction the summit is in. Worse, and actually most often if they don't talk about it, they're most likely to start heading in different directions. Telling that group to focus on the climb would be a disaster; they might focus themselves right off a cliff.

When a team lacks alignment, you'll notice that things are often disorganized and priorities crumble at the slightest change in direction—lethal, at companies where change is the only constant. This is especially true given the creative chaos in early-stage companies, and a team can only safeguard against chaos creep if they're aligned. If not, you'll start to see people drifting back toward their own well-worn paths and what works best for them, instead of the direction the team agreed to take together.

So why, and how, do teams fall out of alignment—or never get aligned in the first place? According to Harvard Business Review, there are four main reasons for continued team misalignment:

1. **Leadership isn't paying attention.** If the company's leaders aren't even aware of the risks of misalignment, they're not likely to recognize it very quickly before disparate teams in their silos dig in deeper and their roads diverge further. Leadership needs to be proactive—*create* alignment, not just hope that it happens.

2. **Alignment is left up to chance.** In other words, no one "owns" alignment. This is something that the team should all own together (and Peak works by

reinforcing everyone's responsibility within the team to work aligned).

3. **Complexity makes alignment harder.** Makes sense; when there are more details to keep track of, teams are more likely to go their own way on the details they work with directly. But just because the business is complex doesn't mean alignment can't be simple!

4. **Activity is mistaken for progress.** This is where the Chicago team was when I worked with them in their first session. They were grinding hard, but getting nowhere. No wonder: they didn't know where they were going in the first place.

Most importantly to a venture-backed company, alignment provides *focus* and *visibility*. In an aligned team, there's no confusion or clutter in the work; everyone has visibility on what their teammates are doing, and teams have visibility on the work of other teams. There's no worrying something isn't getting done—it's clear who's doing what. People are free to focus. All of the stakeholders, from team members themselves to investors and clients, can see and understand what's going on. This means that issues and roadblocks are identified earlier, and new opportunities stand out more clearly.

Peak OS reinforces alignment with the Mission Statement developed by the company's core founders and leaders, and then the first two major activities the team does together at each Annual Session: the Three Year Vision (3YV) and the One Year Plan (1YP).

Let's dive deeper into each of these.

MISSION STATEMENT

In our Peak analogy, we think of the company's Mission Statement as its North Star. These days on an expedition you'd have GPS, obviously, but no matter what happens with your tech, you have the North Star to guide you in the right direction; a company's mission statement acts in the same capacity. It's the organization's guiding light, your highest level Why and How. It provides inspiration for the team and motivation to act.

Typically, the Mission Statement is developed at the founding of the company by the founders themselves or a small, core group of leaders. It's not a team activity, but it's of paramount importance to drill it with the team during Annual Sessions, so here's a rundown of how to create or solidify your Mission Statement so you're certain it's locked in for your team to be inspired by.

The Mission Statement defines the following:

- **The Why.** Why does the organization exist? What is the cause, purpose or belief? The Why is the company's reason for being.

- **The How.** How will you achieve your mission? The How defines how you will successfully achieve or accomplish your cause, purpose, or belief.

- **Why + How.** By combining your Why and How, you'll create your mission statement.

To get started, have the founder, founders, or the small core leadership team members involved in developing the Mission Statement answer these two questions individually:

- What is your company's cause, purpose or belief?

- How do you achieve or accomplish this cause, purpose or belief?

Instruct them to go deeper in their thinking by simply asking why whenever they come up with a statement. For example: "Our purpose is to provide AI-automated screening for common preventable medical conditions." Why? "So that conditions are caught earlier." Why? "So that outcomes are better for patients, and treatment is less expensive overall." You can see how drilling down like this quickly gets to the root of what your organization is actually after as a mission.

When everyone is ready, put a session sheet on the wall and create two columns on it: one titled "Why" and one titled "How". Everyone will share their answers, and you'll write them on the sheet in the appropriate column. Make sure each answer is only a few words long; you want these statements to be clear, concise, and immediately understandable.

With all the statements on the sheet, begin discussion to come up with the final "Why" and "How". This can be done by combining concepts, debating and coming to agreement on eliminating concepts, and merging concepts that are similar (you'll find the last one to be the most common case, and that's a good thing).

Once you have your final "Why" and "How" agreed upon, it's time to combine them to create the mission statement. This part takes some wordsmithing. Work on it as a group, stick to the brevity rule, and make absolutely sure that the final result connects with everyone.

With your mission statement perfected, go share it with the larger team! Some iteration as the mission statement is shared is to be expected, but again, this is not a team activity; this is a decision that truly should be made and owned by the founders/ core leaders of the company.

Meet together for a final session a week or two later to discuss any proposed tweaks and put the final stamp on your mission statement.

THREE YEAR VISION

The Three Year Vision is the first step in getting your team on the same page about the major W's of their work: where they're going, when they'll get there, and what they need to do in order to make it. By acting as a roadmap for all team objectives, it reinforces alignment day after day, week, month, and quarter. It also continuously promotes three major elements of team success: alignment, focus, and accountability.

- **Alignment**: By building a three year vision together, teams have the important conversations that create a stronger collaborative vision.

- **Focus**: Developing a clear vision creates focus which allows teams to make better decisions and focus on the right activities.

- **Accountability**: With clarity and visibility on everyone's role in getting to the peak, everyone's expected results are crystal clear. There's no room for a lack of accountability—so people are accountable for their results, end of story.

You'll create the three year vision once per year, at the Annual Session.

DEFINING FUNCTIONAL AREAS

To start, you and your team will define and align on the functional areas of your organization. Typically, there will be anywhere from five to ten functional areas, depending on the size of the company. And, depending upon your industry or business, you may have one or two additional unique functional areas. For most VC-backed companies, this is how they commonly break down:

- Sales
- Marketing
- Product Management
- Engineering
- Customer Success
- Finance
- Operations
- People

You'll also add to the list the function of Corporate and Capital Development, which is the functional area of the CEO.

As I mentioned before, CEOs in venture-backed teams are the central hub to the organization, managing the board, investors, and team. Within Corporate and Capital Development, their responsibilities break down as follows:

1. Maintaining the vision
2. Building the organization
3. Raising the capital to succeed

Once you have these areas defined, you'll define and align on the owner of each functional area. It's important that each functional area has *one* owner, no more. However, for earlier-stage companies, it's common that one person may be the owner of more than one functional area, for example the CEO also owning Sales, or Product also owning Engineering. But you wouldn't want two people owning, for instance, Sales.

With these two steps completed, we place a session sheet on the wall and get to work.

THE PEAK TEAM DASHBOARD

Peak provides an organization tool called the Peak Team Dashboard, a digital tool accessible by the whole team. It's the central location for all vision, plans, and notes, and is also where you'll operate each Weekly Camp Meeting. It can be used for the leadership team, and each functional area or divisional team can also have their own dashboard—one central place for keeping everyone on the same page.

The Peak Team Dashboard is what we typically use in a Quarterly Session or Annual Session instead of session sheets on the wall. Everyone has their laptops out and is working together in the same organized dashboard.

For the purposes of describing the work of the Peak Team Sessions in this book, however, I've improvised a little to make things easier to visualize while you're reading—that's why you'll read about using session sheets, i.e., big sticky note sheets wall-papering the meeting room. And Peak is, at its heart, simple. You don't need anything more than a notepad and pen to get great work done with your team. In reality, though—you'll use the Peak Team Dashboard. You can access an example of the Peak Team Dashboard by going to this link: *www.collective-genius.com/peak-os-access*, and you can also find a step by step walkthrough of how to use the Dashboard in Peak OS Access.

Title your first session sheet *Three Year Vision—End of Year* (*three years out*). The year in parentheses will be three years out from where you are right now; so if it's 2024, write *End of Year (2026)*. On the sheet, you'll list out each functional area and its owner.

Have the team pull out their prep work. One of the questions they will have worked on as part of prep is about the 3YV. They will get input from their own teams—bottoms-up involvement is important for overall buy-in.

Each functional area leader will share the top three objectives they would like to accomplish three years out in their functional area. As a team, you'll walk through each of these objectives, and discuss and iterate until the team understands and agrees on everyone's objectives, creating team alignment. It's likely that the owner of each functional area will lead the conversation when it's concerning their area of ownership, but it's crucial that *everyone* participates in the discussion of all objectives so that the whole team has input and is aligned to the objectives of each functional area. Write the defined objectives of each functional area under the area on the session sheet.

When you're done, you'll transfer all the information on the session sheets into the Peak Teams Dashboard. Once the team has completed and aligned on each objective you're ready to move on to the 1YP.

ONE YEAR PLAN

Once your team has fully mapped out their 3YV, it's time to get a little more granular and answer the question, "What does success look like by the end of the year?"

For each functional area, you'll ask the question, "What does success look like for [functional area] by the end of the year?" You'll go function by function and build out the objectives.

Similarly to how you did the 3YV, place one or two session sheets on the wall (or as many as you'll need to write out all the functional areas). Title the first sheet *One Year Plan—EOY (current year)*. So, let's still say you're in 2024; it'll read *EOY (2024)*. List out all the functional areas of the business and each owner's name. Have the team pull out their prep work they did with each of their teams and plug in three to five objectives in each of their functional areas. These objectives should represent what they feel success looks like in their functional area by the end of the year.

They can be metric-based objectives (KPIs) or non-metric based objectives. Encourage each functional area to have at least one metric-based objective that is their "Guiding KPI" (we'll go deeper into KPIs in Part Three).

Again, each functional leader walks through each of their objectives, allowing the team to ask questions and discuss and make any changes to align the objectives cross-functionally with the other functional areas. For example, qualified marketing leads should align with sales metrics; product epics should align with engineering releases; the finance runway and budget should align with the hiring plans of the People functional area.

In creating objectives, it's important to find the balance between the priority and importance of each one. It's common for a discussion to center on one "big" objective which ends up overshadowing the rest—one objective to rule them all. For example, the Head of Sales might say something like, "All we need to do is $12 million in sales this year; that's all we need to hit."

If this happens, encourage your team to go deeper. *Okay, but what do you need to do to get that done?* Hire a sales team, create better onboarding, maybe get a more efficient CRM? Make sure they're thinking deeply into not just the *what*, but the *how*.

For instance, the Head of Engineering might state, "Our objective is to release the product." Well, sure. But what will get you there? Pull up the product roadmap to review major milestones. Maybe an objective is actually *building* a product roadmap. Maybe you need to implement new tech to push the product out.

Or an example in the CEO's functional area, Corporate and Capital Development, you may have an objective like, "Raise a Series A of $25 million." But what does that actually look like, and what do you need to do to get there? What kind of VCs are you looking at? What type of funding are you looking for? At what valuation? What's your Board going to look like after funding?

These discussions don't need to get too deep; the aim of these questions is just to make sure the team is taking a full look at each potential objective and selecting the most important ones.

Again, it's about striking the right balance of goals versus granularity. You don't want to get lost in the weeds, but your team needs to agree on the steps they're actually going to take up the mountain. Your goal here is to stick to what is most important to accomplish and give the team visibility on.

In creating the 3YV and 1YP, you're giving your team a roadmap they can habitually refer to throughout the expedition to ensure that they're on track not only individually, or by functional area, but as a team moving cohesively together in the same direction. And that's all alignment is, really; forward progress in the same direction toward a shared goal destination. Creating a habit of adherence to your map is what will reinforce sticking together in the right direction.

In an aligned team, priorities are clear, which makes cross-collaboration across teams smoother. Everyone is aligned on who owns what, so there's no overlapping or gaps in the work. And when you get all the information into the Peak Team Dashboard, it's clean, easy to follow, and keeps the team anchored.

Most importantly, alignment promotes accountability and ownership, which are huge drivers for trust. When everyone understands their objectives—as well as those of their teammates—they are more likely to take ownership of their work and be accountable for their actions. This will supercharge the engagement, motivation, and commitment to the company's goals.

EXAMPLES

THREE YEAR VISION: EARLY STAGE EXAMPLE

Corporate and Capital Development (CEO): Arianna

- Close 15m Series A
- Restructure Board of Directors
- Establish International GTM Strategy

Engineering: Carlos

- Define and Improve Mean Time to Resolution
- Reduce Technical Debt by 30%
- Outsource Corporate IT

Sales: Arianna

- 3.5m ARR
- 50 Clients
- Onboard Head of Sales and Scale Team

Customer Success - Alex

- Churn Rate < 0.06
- Implement Customer Success Framework 2.0
- Complete HubSpot Implementation

Marketing: Drew

- CAC < 1,100
- Google Analytics & HubSpot Implemented
- Launch Paid ROI Advertising Campaigns

Finance and Operations: Mei

- Enhance Forecasting Accuracy and Budgeting Processes
- Develop Strategy and Plan to Increase Profit Margins by 15%
- Onboard CFO

Product Management: Sophia

- 12 Month Rolling Product Roadmap
- Establish System for Analyzing Product Usage Data
- Launch Consumer Product Council

People: Mei

- Coordinate Annual and Quarterly Company Meetings
- Define and Implement Employee Culture Score
- Hire and Manage Internal Recruiter

THREE YEAR VISION: LATE STAGE EXAMPLE

Corporate and Capital Development (CEO): Perry

- Close 105m Series C
- Implement Acquisition Strategy Map
- Uplift and Restructure Board of Directors

Engineering: Julia

- DevSecOps Environment Implemented
- Data Science Team Fully Operational
- Engineering Hubs Based in SF and LA

Business Operations: Skyler

- Open Regional Office to Support Infrastructure Growth
- Scale Operations with Three International Markets
- Uplift Corporate Systems and Processes to Support 50% Increase Subscriptions

Data Analytics and Business Intelligence: Julia

- Robust Data Infrastructure Supporting 50% Increase in Data Volume
- Establish Data Quality and Data Governance Standard Fully Supported Feature Oriented Data-Driven Culture

Sales: Adi

- 42m ARR
- Secure 32 Fortune 500 Clients
- Sales, AM and BD Teams Integrated and Operational

Customer Success: Nikolay

- Churn Rate < 0.05
- Customer Strategy Team Operational
- ZenDesk Integrations Complete

Marketing: Stephen

- LTV:CAC Ratio > 5:1
- Onboard and Integrate CMO
- Expand into Three New Verticals

Finance: Whitney

- Workday Financial Management and Planning Launched
- Define Capital Structure Strategy to Support Growth Objectives
- Improve Cash Conversion Cycle by 15%

Product Management: Mala	People: Jax
• 12 Month Rolling Product Roadmap • Gartner Magic Quadrant Leader Status • Implement Quarterly Product Council Meetings	• Employee Health Score > 9.2 • Execute Leadership and Company Gatherings Cadence • Head of People Onboarded

ONE YEAR PLAN: EARLY STAGE EXAMPLE

Corporate and Capital Development (CEO): Arianna	Engineering: Carlos
• Close 2.1m Seed Round • Execute on Investor Pipeline System • Recruit GTM Focused BOD Member • Develop and Execute on Hiring Plan • Complete Techstars Program	• Launch 3 Live Product Releases • Implement a Scalability Plan Supporting a 400% Increase in User Load • Reduce Post-release Bugs by 50% Through New Testing Protocols • Uplift Engineering Visibility with Product and Engineering Meeting Reporting • Hire 1 Front-end and 2 Back-end Developers

Sales: Arianna	Customer Success: Alex
• 650k ARR • Document Sales Methodology and Process • Implement Salesforce.com • Onboard Sales Executive and BDR • Develop 1,500 Prospective Companies List	• Churn Rate < 0.06 • Customer Success framework implemented • Create Sales to Customer Success Hand-Off Process • Define Future Customer Success Tool Functionality

Marketing: Drew

- Define and Measure CAC
- Test and Measure 5 Marketing Campaigns
- Execute Content Marketing Strategy
- Identify and Document Ideal Customer Profile

Finance and Operations: Mei

- Secure Fractional CFO & Accountant
- Implement FreshBooks
- Process R&D Software Development Tax Credits

Product Management: Sophia

- 110 Monthly Active Users
- Release 3 Month Rolling Product Roadmap
- Document Product Management Intake Process
- Create and Launch Internal Product Advisory Council

People: Mei

- Hire and Manage External Technical Recruiters
- Document and Implement Recruiting Process
- Coordinate Annual and Quarterly Offsite Meetings
- Implement Employee Benefits with Sequoia

ONE YEAR PLAN: LATE STAGE EXAMPLE

Corporate and Capital Development (CEO): Perry

- Close 46m Series B
- Secure 3 Strategic Investors
- Implement Leadership Team Talent Mapping
- Expand 3 New Market Strategic Partnerships
- Support Strategic Revenue Efforts

Engineering: Julia

- 6 Product Releases Live
- Complete Migration of All Services Running on Legacy Systems
- Document and Measure Increased Data Security Systems
- Implement Multi-factor Authentication for all Users
- Standup Data and Analytics Teams

Operations: Skyler

- Increase Operational Efficiency by 10%
- Implement Quarterly and Weekly Team Cadence
- Develop and Activate Operations Plan
- Refresh Data Room

Customer Success: Nikolay

- NPS > 70
- Churn Rate < 0.06
- Customer Success Framework 2.0 Implemented
- CX Platform Defined and Implemented
- Onboard Director of CX

Sales: Adi

- 15m ARR
- Secure 10 Fortune 500 Clients
- Implement CRM with Sales Funnel Tracking
- Launch 5m Partner Program
- Hire 5 BDRs and 1 Strategic Partnership Rep

Finance: Whitney

- Maintain > 20 Monthly Runway
- Complete and Enhance Annual Financial Modeling
- Update Documentation Process for R&D Tax Credits
- Onboard Corporate Controller
- Open New SF Office Space

Marketing: Stephen

- LTV:CAC Ratio > 3:1
- 110 MQLs
- Launch 3 Campaigns Tied to New Product Features
- Complete Marketo Implementation
- Develop and Track Lead Generation Process

Product Management: Mala

- < 95% Weekly Product Feature Usage
- Gartner Magic Quadrant Visionary Status
- Release 12 Month Rolling Product Roadmap
- Define New Product Feature Scoring System

People: Jax

- Employee Health Score > 8.8
- Launch Employee Core Value Awards
- Implement Loxo ATS
- Document Recruiting Process

FIVE

NIGHT AND DAY

"If you don't know where you are going,
you'll end up someplace else."

–YOGI BERRA

"WOW. I CAN'T BELIEVE WE WERE MISSING SOMETHING so simple."

The CEO's remark was mirrored on the faces of most people in the room; they were feeling good, and the energy was high. I was still unsure about the Head of Product, and would be interested to see how he progressed by the next session.

A positive consequence to teams finding greater alignment is that it helps everyone get where they want to go. People who just aren't wanting to *work* on a team, people who prefer to execute as an isolated functional island rather than a plugged-in piece of a machine, are able to hide amidst misalignment. The lack of clarity, the confusion on priorities, the spinning wheels and grinding hard only to stand still—they all act as a cloak for someone who just wants to do their own thing and not be challenged in their movements.

But add in a key tool like a 3YV and 1YP that gets everyone aligned, and gets objectives transparent, visible, and trackable, and suddenly they can't hide anymore. It creates accountability.

I knew I'd be interested to get the update from the CEO the following quarter on how the team's progress on the 1YP was going—especially from a people perspective.

As we wrapped up that day's session, everyone was smiling and in a good mood. Through the day's work on the vision, plan, and objectives, they'd realized that they'd all been trying to go fast in ten different directions. Having the clarity of the vision and plan right in front of their faces was incredibly energizing; they could finally speak the same language, operate as a team. If you've ever played sports, you'll know the magic feeling when a team actually clicks into teamwork, rather than just a bunch of talented people running around after a ball. There's a feeling of flow and unity that comes from clarity and communication.

After the session, I checked in with the CEO on FaceTime as I was Ubering (I'd learned my lesson with the morning's freezing trek) back to my hotel.

"That was amazing," she said. "For the first time in a long time, I felt like everyone was on the same page. The vision and plan for the future feel so tangible. I feel like everyone's going to be able to just *run*."

Her whole energy had changed. This was the beginning of coming out of the CEO Stress Spiral.

We made a plan to check in after four weeks of Weekly Camp Meetings (which you'll learn more about in Part Four: Communication).

And sure enough, during that check-in, a change had already been made.

First, the good stuff. The entire company embraced the 3YV and 1YP; it was tangible down to each team. Finally, the entire organization was all moving in the same direction up the mountain.

FILLING A KEY ROLE

The whole team was now very aware of the lack of clarity they'd been working with before, from the perspective of their employees, customers, candidates they were recruiting, and even their investors. Before the session, no one had been able to give a solid rundown of exactly where they were going and what they needed to do to get there.

"Seeing how we were working before compared to how we're working now... it's like night and day," the CEO told me. "It's like everyone has a perfect elevator pitch at the ready for what they're doing. And it all makes sense together as one cohesive picture."

With their vision, plan, and the communication around their work clearly defined, they saw their first major win at three weeks post session when they landed their dream candidate for CRO—a role they'd been trying to hire for over a year. It hadn't been obvious to them before why they were having so much trouble hiring for the role. Now, it was obvious that they had been unable to attract the best talent because no one in their company could clearly communicate their mission.

Now that they could communicate about their expedition, the right people wanted to join the climb.

CLARITY OF FOCUS

With their new clarity, and with a clear understanding of what success looked like by the end of the year for each functional area, it was much easier for each team to see exactly where they needed to focus. The CEO told me that in a recent Weekly Camp Meeting, the Head of Sales had said, "It's like we have a lighthouse actually guiding us with a clear beacon instead of wandering around in a fog."

Gone were the days of people "working just to work", spinning their wheels and grinding on tasks that didn't move the needle. It was undeniable to everyone what they should be focusing on. It was also easier to keep track of where everyone else was focusing, leading to better alignment on priorities across the board. For example, when the CMO and Head of Engineering actually had visibility into what each other were doing, opportunities for optimization popped up that they were able to take advantage of.

They weren't a Frankenstein mishmash of talented individuals and their individual plans anymore; they were a unified team getting win after win *together*.

CONSISTENT ACCOUNTABILITY

With everyone's objectives "up on the board", so to speak, and Peak reinforcing the habit of continual alignment to those objectives, there was really no way for anyone *not* to get things done. It would be immediately obvious if they were getting off track.

Rather than making everyone paranoid, though, the unity of the 3YV and 1YP created more confidence in their ability to succeed and be accountable—and even more importantly, to lead their own teams into the habit of accountability. Being aligned and clear on the vision and plan, having a clear picture of success, and going through the weekly habit of communicating issues and re-tracking to their 3YV/1YP actually gave everyone a huge amount of relief. They were clear where they stood and no longer felt like they were throwing darts in the dark, hoping they were landing in the right spot.

At the end of the day, everyone wants to do a good job. And everyone wants to be accountable for their results. Give a team the tools and habits to do that, and they'll be more energized than you can imagine. The momentum your team will experience from win after win will be addictive.

"But," the CEO told me on our four-week check-in, "as you can probably guess, we did need to make a change. And actually, he made it for himself; our Head of Product resigned a week ago."

I've seen time and time again that Peak tends to make things work out for the best. When changes to the team happen, it doesn't surprise me.

The CEO told me that there were no hard feelings on either side. The Head of Product was just not comfortable with the new collaboration habits of the team, and didn't really align with the direction of the organization.

"I feel like Peak gave both of us a big gift," she said. "He figured out the kind of environment that would make him happiest, and he went after it—I think his new role is actually a salary and title bump for him. And for us, the super clear alignment and communication made it so obvious so quickly that something wasn't working. We didn't have to waste months or years stewing in discomfort, letting resentment and conflict grow. It was a fast, obvious change. We're both a lot happier now, thanks to Peak."

CASE STUDY: MATCHSTICK VENTURES

I conducted this interview with Ryan Broshar,
Founder and General Partner for Matchstick Ventures

Every business, from startups to established companies, should have a clear vision and plan. This plan should not only set targets but should also be the roadmap for the year. It keeps everyone, including VCs, on the same page. For VCs, this ensures their portfolio of startups is streamlined, making it easier to relay updates to their own investors.

In my time as a VC, I've identified a noticeable gap at most companies: a robust operating system. Many VC-backed companies struggle to measure their performance and define future goals. It's surprising how many don't have some form of systematic operational discipline.

Many traditional business operating systems advocate for business owners to step back, hire someone else to run the daily operations, and focus on being a "visionary." In the venture-backed space, this isn't practical. The role of a CEO in a startup is critical; they can't simply be a "visionary." They're accountable to a board and a group of stakeholders. CEOs often wear multiple hats, from operations to development and everything in between. If a startup's founder says they want to step back and hire someone else to run their business within a few years, that's a red flag for me as an investor. The passion and drive to grow the business should be obvious and authentic. The determination to work through challenges with limited resources is what sets successful startups apart.

We've always advised our startups to set annual and quarterly goals, emphasizing progress over motion—but for a while, we found ourselves distracted by every new opportunity, almost like moths to a flame. This scattered approach wasn't what we were advising our portfolio companies to adopt, and it was high time we practiced what we preached. We recognized the necessity of long-term planning, especially given the elongated timelines in the VC space. That's when we brought in Peak.

Adopting Peak OS was transformative. By the year's end, we could see the milestones we'd achieved, boosting our confidence and gearing us up for even bigger challenges. For our portfolio companies, their performance became so much clearer when they began discussing progress in real, tangible metrics rather than bringing us vague updates. This shift in dialogue and mindset marked a significant growth point for both us and our portfolios.

Investors don't want to be taken by surprise; they appreciate foresight and a well-structured plan. It all boils down to measurable accountability. When we have a system in place, we can set clear goals for the coming month, quarter, or even year. And yes, sometimes we miss the mark, either overshooting or falling short. But that's okay, because it starts a conversation about why. The discussion itself helps us improve.

There have been challenges, of course. When we tried introducing this level of accountability to the companies we work with, some resisted. Not everyone appreciates the structure. Some creatives feel boxed in, preferring to keep their attention just on what's happening tomorrow rather than the entire year. But in my experience, the best entrepreneurs can paint a vivid picture of the future. They have a clear vision.

In business, it's not just about what you're doing today. It's about where you're headed tomorrow. And to get there, you need a map, a vision, and the will to follow through.

PART 3

SYMBIOSIS

SIX

WHEN MEASURING FEELS MORE LIKE GUESSING

"Measure what is measurable, and make
measurable what is not so."

—GALILEO GALILEI

T WAS A BEAUTIFUL FALL AFTERNOON IN NEW YORK, AND
the streets were full of people enjoying the crisp October air.
I decided that an Uber from Brooklyn into Manhattan was
worth it to avoid the crowds in the subway. As the Prius that
had picked me up slowly crept through busy streets toward

the bridge, I scrolled my phone with one thumb, reading through the email I'd received from the person I was headed to Manhattan to meet: the CEO of a seed-stage EdTech company I'd been introduced to by an investor in the company.

His email giving me background on his team had a distinct tone of frustration—one I'd heard a lot from CEOs in my work, and still hear to this day. One line in particular stood out to me.

We've tried goal setting, OKRs, and tons of other methods to get on the same page, but nothing sticks. We always get off track and stop using whatever tool it is. And each team ends up just going back to whatever way they're used to doing things. It feels like we've tried everything and nothing works.

This tracked with the answers to the Peak Team Surveys I'd collected. The responses showed a team that was excited about the mission, but—much like the Chicago team from Part Two—was moving in ten different directions all at once.

When I arrived at Birch Coffee, I saw the company's CEO sitting at a table by the window. After ordering an Americano and joining him, we got right down to business.

"Have you ever been sailing?" he asked me, and I nodded. "Okay, then you'll get this."

He proceeded to describe a team adrift on a boat with no sail and no rudder. "I don't feel we have control of the business. We're paddling like maniacs, but we're just drifting with the current and *hoping* it pulls us in the right direction."

"But you haven't always felt like this, right?" I asked. "There was a time when things felt in control."

He nodded. "Definitely. When we first started out, we got wins really quickly. We worked well together as a team. But now..." He sighed. "I don't know if it's just the scale we're at, but what we did before isn't working anymore. Our results have flatlined. And right when we actually have the capital to go faster and grow!"

The company had graduated from a large accelerator program and had enjoyed immediate growth and funding right out of the gate. But now, while trying to raise their Series A, they were suddenly missing their projections quarter after quarter, constantly having to explain and re-explain to the Board what wasn't working.

"It just feels like we don't know what we're doing. Which is *not* how we started. But we can't find that early success again. I'm starting to wonder if it was just luck."

I reassured him enthusiastically—maybe a little too enthusiastically, thanks to the caffeine content of the twelve-dollar artisanal espresso I was sipping—that luck had nothing to do with it. They'd smashed goals once before, and they could do it again.

"Truly, I see this all the time in companies at every level in the game," I told him. "It's not just seed stage where this happens; I've seen this at Series B, C, and D. I even just worked with a public company that had this same problem."

"And what *is* the problem?" he asked.

I pulled up the email he'd sent me and read him the part that had stood out to me before. "You said you've tried tons of models and nothing sticks. So, what are you guys using to set goals and measure progress right now, then?"

As I suspected: *nothing.* "We have revenue targets that we share with investors, and we have a view of our budget and runway. But other than that, we don't really have metrics we're tracking. I'd call what we're doing more like 'financial planning' than actually tracking KPIs."

"Okay," I said. "Then that's where we start."

He looked a little uncertain. "I don't know. I've tried getting buy-in from the team on metrics, but when we kept setting KPIs and missing them by a mile, they really lost trust in that kind of tracking."

The next day, at the session in the team's small but comfortable Midtown office, this was confirmed right away.

I asked the team: "What has worked and not worked with OKRs and KPIs in the past?"

The company's CMO raised her hand firmly. "Every time we try to set metrics, we just end up being *way* off. Why even set them when it's a total guess?"

"Okay," I said. "And how about OKRs?"

Now it was the Head of Sales who answered. "I'm totally bought in to doing OKRs when reading about it in books, but none of those books tell you how to actually implement them. When we've tried it in the past, it just feels like our OKRs must not be dialed in, because it only takes a week or two before everything's off track."

I asked her to tell me how her team currently measured success. She described a half-baked goal-setting method I knew was different from what was being used by other teams in the company. One by one, I called on each team lead in the room and asked them to describe how they were defining and measuring success. Sure enough, they *all* had different systems, and nobody was confident in any of them.

"Let me ask you something different," I said to the group. "Do you feel like a team?"

They all looked at each other from their spots around the conference room table. I could tell no one wanted to state the obvious.

The CEO had no such reluctance, though. "I think I speak for everyone when I say that no, we don't feel like a team. We used to. But we don't anymore."

I nodded. "Do you feel unified as a company?" I continued.

Emboldened by their CEO's candor, they shook their heads.

"Do you trust each other to get the results you're accountable for?"

The CMO spoke up this time. "I don't think it's that we don't trust, I think it's that we don't know or understand what anyone else is doing. I *know* we're all grinding, but we can't tell if anything we're doing is working or not."

There it was. She'd found it. That's how perfectly she had described what it looks like when one of the core behaviors of high-functioning VC-backed teams is missing: symbiosis.

Symbiosis is something that's hard to point to, but when a team is *not* operating in symbiosis, it's obvious. For a team to be symbiotic, they need to understand where they're going and exactly what each of them are going to contribute in order to get there. They start the process by building their 3YV and 1YP, but they need to continue down that path by defining what they need to do to succeed—which consequently measures if they're on course.

Symbiosis is simple: it's when everyone is working together in unity, thriving in an environment of trust and respect. Everyone is trusted to execute their unique role and achieve their agreed-upon results; everyone trusts their teammates to have their back and not let the team down. And as a thriving team, everyone is driving toward a shared purpose and goals that have been clearly defined and communicated. The team works together collectively to successfully achieve the mission and vision of the organization. The company wins, and therefore everyone wins.

Could I have called this core team behavior "synergy"? Sure. But that word has been overused to death, and it also doesn't connote the living, breathing feeling of a symbiotic relationship. Symbiosis is about people, and it can't be manufactured.

It also can't be assumed. In fact, most teams I've worked with don't start out working in symbiosis. The mere fact of being on a team together doesn't mean people know how to create an environment that feels like a team.

Symbiosis is built on respect—respect for the role each individual plays within their team, and respect for the role each team plays within the organization as a whole. Even if each team within a company has achieved symbiosis, the company as a whole needs to achieve it, as a team of teams. All too often, I work with companies where Sales isn't talking to Engineering, Marketing has no idea what Finance is doing, and so on. Giving periodic updates where people drone on and on isn't the answer. Teams that work well within their own discipline need to collaborate cross-functionally as well. The objectives of the company rely on it.

This team of people was definitely aligned on their mission. They were clear on what they were trying to accomplish together. They knew where their peak was and the big picture of what they needed to do to get there.

But in trying to climb the mountain, they weren't sure what each person's individual contribution was supposed to look like, so they had no way of trusting that what they were all doing day to day was actually gaining them any elevation.

"We have a clear picture of our 1YP. The next step in the process is to zoom closer and build out the next 90 days together," I told them. "We're going to build Objectives and Key Results, OKRs, for this upcoming quarter."

I could see skepticism written on a few of their faces. Seeing this often makes me laugh, because time and time again, it turns out that the *most* skeptical people tend to become the biggest advocates of Peak. And that just makes it fun.

SEVEN

THE WHAT AND THE HOW

"I am a member of a team, and I rely on the team, I
defer to it and sacrifice for it, because the team,
not the individual, is the ultimate champion."

–MIA HAMM

T HE THREE YEAR VISION AND ONE YEAR PLAN GET EVERY-
one on the team *aligned*—on where you're going, when
you'll get there, and the big picture of what you need to do
to make it happen.

To build and reinforce symbiosis, you need to create ways
for the team to create wins together. That's what we're doing
with OKRs and KPIs. We're not only creating waypoints up the

mountain, ways for everyone to track progress and measure the success of the expedition while they're hiking, but we're also building the capabilities within the organization to make it happen: unity, trust, and cohesiveness with every waypoint the team hits. In a company like yours, where teams are especially interconnected and inter-reliant, this couldn't be more important.

OBJECTIVES AND KEY RESULTS (OKRS)

Most of you reading this book will likely be *very* familiar with the term OKR, but for those who might not be, here's a quick history of this tried and true business tool.

Back in the 1950s, Peter Drucker invented Management by Objectives (MBO). This early predecessor to OKRs was taken and run with by Andrew Grove at Intel in 1968; he further developed MBO into what more resembles the OKR framework we know today. Then, in 1974, John Doerr joined Intel, learned the OKR framework, and took it with him as he became a well-known tech investor. He spread OKRs to many of what have become today's biggest tech companies, among them Google, Apple, and Amazon.

An OKR is made up of an Objective and one or more Key Results.

- **Objective**: Simply put, something you want to achieve. These are goals and intentions—significant, concrete, action-oriented, and, ideally, inspirational to the team. The objective is the *what*.

- *Key Result*: This is a measurable milestone under an Objective. Effective key results follow the SMART goal framework; they're specific, measurable, attainable, realistic (yet aggressive), and timely. The key result is *how*.

You'll build your Quarterly OKRs every 90 days with your team. You're going to start by building three to five objectives with key results that create focus and accountability as a team, then additional objectives for each functional area of the company.

This part of the session can feel long, and it's intensive, focused work. When I run sessions, I build in regular breaks and check-in often to make sure everyone stays engaged. Just like when you created your 3YV and 1YP, it's crucially important that the entire team participates, the *entire* time. OKRs that don't have full team ownership and buy-in will actually work *against* building symbiosis.

DEFINING OKRS

Two to three weeks prior to the session, each team member is given prep work to unpack their thoughts together with their teams. This integrates everyone into the process, sometimes referred to as "bottoms-up planning."

To build the objectives:

1. One by one, have each person share one objective they believe should be among the top three to five objectives for the quarter and explain why. The "why" is very important—this is your opportunity to advocate for why this objective should be one of the top three to five objectives.

2. Go around the room, sharing one objective per person at a time, until everyone feels the top objectives are listed.

Then, reduce them to the most important objectives:

1. Ask the team if any objectives should be removed because they shouldn't be a focus for the quarter; discuss and remove.

2. Ask the team if any of the objectives should be moved to a functional objective and don't need to be a top team objective; discuss and move.

3. Ask the team if there are any smaller objectives that could be combined or might act as a key result of another objective listed; discuss and combine.

Complete each step one at a time and repeat if necessary, until the team agrees on three to five final objectives. It's best to narrow them down to three; if not, you can vote (but I find it best to work your way down to three or five objectives versus voting).

Here are some best practices to help guide you in creating your objectives:

- **Clear Objectives**: Each objective should articulate what you aim to achieve. It should be expressed in a way that makes it easy to determine if it has been accomplished.

- **Right Size**: Each objective should be appropriately sized—more than a quick task, but achievable within 90 days.

- **Combine Similar Small Objectives**: If you have smaller objectives that are alike, group them under a larger, appropriately sized objective. For instance, if you have "create new product one-pagers" and "update product information on the website," you could combine these under "Update Product Marketing Resources" and note the specifics.

- **Avoid grouping medium or large projects:** For example, don't combine "Implement Sales CRM" with "Create Sales Process," as each could take 60 to 90 days. Don't overload your team with mega-objectives that aren't achievable in the upcoming quarter.

Now that your Top Three Team Objectives are set, you can round out the OKRs by creating Key Results for each objective. Put another session sheet on the wall and write down the first Team Objective. For each one, define the following elements:

- **Ownership:** Each objective will have an owner. Write their name down next to the objective.

- **The *How*:** For each objective, ask the team, "How will we accomplish this objective?" For each action they name, make sure it's SMART (Specific, Measurable, Achievable, Relevant, and Time-Bound), then write it down as a key result.

- **Key Result Owners:** Each key result will have an owner, just like objectives. Write a name down next to each key result.

- **The *When***: For each key result, define the date it will be completed and write it next to the key result.

- **Others**: Define who else you may need to help support in getting that key result completed.

Repeat the above process to define at least three key results for each of your top three to five Team Objectives. Once these are locked in, you're ready to review the Functional Objectives. The number of functional objectives you define for each team will largely be guided by what the owner of that functional area feels confident their team can accomplish in 90 days.

Just like when you created the 3YV and 1YP, it's likely that the discussion of objectives for each functional area will be led by the owner of that area—but everyone needs to participate regardless. It's rare that an OKR would exist in a vacuum; an OKR from one functional area will likely impact or be dependent on OKRs from other functional areas. Part of building symbiosis is building trust, so it's important that everyone fully understands how their priorities intersect with those of their fellow teams.

We typically only discuss a rough draft of the functional objectives in the session. We let each team assess the team OKRs then adjust their functional objectives. At the next Weekly Camp Meeting, they share and discuss their functional objectives.

THE DIFFERENCE WITH PEAK OKRS

Traditional Key Results often measure just the success of accomplishing an objective. With Peak OKRs, we go deeper. We discuss and define *how* we'll achieve the objective. This added layer of definition clarifies what we all need to collectively do, fostering a sense of symbiosis. Also, traditional OKRs aren't always anchored in the organization's mission, vision, or plan. They're often created in a vacuum, focusing on immediate tasks without considering the bigger picture or end goal.

Another distinction of Peak OKRs is that they're implemented at every level of the organization, unlike traditional methods where only a few objectives trickle down. This approach provides every team, from the leadership team to functional, divisional, and all other teams, with a clear focus, further promoting symbiosis throughout the whole company.

KEY PERFORMANCE INDICATORS (KPIS)

Building the core behavior of symbiosis takes practice. It takes your team pulling together and advancing on your goals unified as one, and working together in efficient and effective rhythms. A team operating in symbiosis, much like an all-star sports team, looks almost choreographed. They're in sync, and they're kept in sync with trust and accountability.

In *The 4 Disciplines of Execution*, Chris McChesney, Sean Covey, and Jim Huling write, "Great teams know, at every moment, whether or not they are winning. They must know, or they cannot make the right decisions about what to do next. The scoreboard is the single most powerful element of a game. It motivates the players to win."

Not only that, but more frequent wins bring your team together in shared accomplishment. And being able to see exactly where their finish line is will actually motivate them further. A 2006 study by behavioral scientist Oleg Urminksy gave birth to the Goal Gradient Theory, which shows that humans are more motivated to work on a goal the closer they are to achieving it. Put another way, you run faster when you can see the finish line in front of you.

Key Performance Indicators (KPIs) are how your team will assess performance and stack up those wins. KPIs define where you want to get to, and are leading indicators to measure progress. They also act as an indicator of staying on course; the data you measure will tell you if you need to course correct at any point during the quarter.

Start small, but *start*—even if you're making guesses when you first start out. By setting KPIs, you will track them. By tracking them, you'll learn about the business. By learning, you'll start to project the future more and more accurately. And as you continue to learn and understand your metrics, you'll master your business and dominate your market.

Here's how to define KPIs:

- Typically you'll want to pick one guiding KPI per functional area when you build the 1YP. As a team scales and grows, and the understanding of the business increases, more KPIs will be added. At early and late stages, though, keep it simple.

- From your 1YP, pull out three to five Team KPIs. Because it's from your 1YP, the metrics will be annual measures—for example, "$15 million ARR", "3 Product Releases", etc.

- Break down those annual KPIs over four quarters. The $15m ARR may scale up each quarter, such as $2m, $3m, $4m, and $6m, reaching the annual $15m; the 3 product releases translate to 1 release per quarter, with a break one quarter. (Note: These KPIs will also help inform your objectives, as the question will naturally arise, "What do we need to do to hit $6m in ARR this quarter?")

THE WHAT AND THE HOW

- Write down the name of the owner next to each KPI. Make sure there's an owner.

- As with the rest of Peak—make sure the whole team is involved! Nothing kills buy-in on KPIs faster than lacking full team buy-in. No one wants to feel beholden to a goal they weren't part of setting. Similar to OKRs, you'll list the KPIs, discuss each one, and iterate if needed.

Add your KPIs to the Peak Team Dashboard.

When it comes to both OKRs and KPIs, remember that data doesn't lie, and your team needs to understand how they stack up as they're executing on their objectives.

KPIs can provide focus for the entire organization. They can be broken down to suit any functional or divisional area within an organization, creating focus for teams at any level. This clarity allows teams to collaborate and work towards shared goals successfully. Teams that consistently track and iterate on their KPIs develop a deeper understanding of the mechanics and levers of the business; they come to grasp what truly moves the needle.

KPIs afford us the opportunity to gain data insights, aiding in informed decision-making. They not only alert you when you're deviating from your path but also provide insights that can help chart new courses. This data-driven approach leads to more effective decision-making.

Having proper metrics that gauge our progress is invaluable both to the internal team and external stakeholders like investors. It offers a means to communicate your current position and the direction in which you're heading.

You'll track and measure your KPIs on a weekly, monthly, and quarterly basis. As you get more data in, and as you understand your KPIs more deeply, you'll also get a better understanding of what exactly they impact across the organization.

Finally, measurement is itself a skill you can improve on. Just by tracking metrics, your team will actually get better at understanding how success is measured, and you'll likely as a team fine-tune your KPIs as the quarters progress.

A common point of pushback I hear on metrics or KPIs is that it's a form of micromanagement. That couldn't be further from the truth, and it's important to discuss *why* you're measuring these very specific indicators with your team. Make sure they understand that KPIs allow the team to discover the data and insights to win over and over again.

Almost every team I've worked with waited way too long to start defining and measuring KPIs. This is where I'll remind you not to let perfect be the enemy of good. Like with all things Peak, just *start*. It doesn't need to be perfect—and it never will be, but with time, you'll get closer.

EXAMPLES

TEAM OKRs: EARLY STAGE

OBJECTIVE ONE
Close 2.1m Seed Round: Arianna

- *Key Result One*: Create Investor Pipeline: Arianna—1/10
- *Key Result Two*: Message Investor Pipeline to Tier One Network: Arianna—1/31
- *Key Result Three*: Complete 25 Investor Meetings: Arianna—2/30

OBJECTIVE TWO
Launch Reporting Product Module: Carlos

- *Key Result One*: Complete and Approve Product Requirements: Sophia—1/09
- *Key Result Two*: Technical and User Testing Completed: Carlos—2/12
- *Key Result Three*: User Testing Completed: Carlos—2/25
- *Key Result Four*: Launch Product Module: Carlos—3/02
- *Key Result Five*: Gather and Share User Feedback: Alex—3/30

OBJECTIVE THREE
Identify and Document Ideal Customer Profile: Drew

- *Key Result One*: Identify List of Our 30 Best Customers: Arianna—1/15
- *Key Result Two*: Analyze Customer Characteristics and Identify Common Patterns: Drew—2/15
- *Key Result Three*: Create Top Five Customer Personas: Drew—3/15
- *Key Result Four*: Document and Share the ICP Results with Leadership Team: Drew—3/20

FUNCTIONAL OBJECTIVES: EARLY STAGE

Corporate and Capital Development Objectives

- Identify Three Potential GTM Focused BOD Members—Arianna: 3/31

Sales Objectives

- 240k ARR Closed—Arianna: 3/31
- Implement Phase One of Salesforce.com Implementation—Ryan: 3/31
- Onboard Sales Executive—Mei: 2/28

Marketing Objectives

- Launch New Website—Drew: 3/31
- Test and Measure 1 New Marketing Campaign—Drew: 3/31
- Launch 15 Social Media Posts—Drew 3/31
- Implement Process to Define CAC—Drew 3/31

Product Objectives

- 85 Monthly Active Users—Sophia 3/31
- Document Product Security Requirements:—Sophia: 3/15
- Identify the 5 Members for the Internal Product Advisory Council and Meeting Cadence—Sophia 2/15

Engineering Objectives

- Database Migration Complete—Carlos 3/31
- Hire three back-end engineers—Carlos: 2/15

Customer Success Objectives

- Churn Rate < 0.10—Alex: 3/31
- Define Customer Success Playbook—Alex: 2/15
- Define Customer Success Monthly Metrics—Alex: 3/15

Finance, Operations and People Objectives

- Complete Audit—Mei: 2/15
- Build and Approve Financial Plan—Mei: 3/15
- Complete EOY Tax Project—Mei: 3/31

TEAM OKRs: LATE STAGE

OBJECTIVE ONE
Design and Launch 5m Partner Program: Adi

- *Key Result*: Define and Present Ideal Partner Profile Tiers: Stephen—01/10
- *Key Result*: Book 75 Tier 1 Meetings with the 250 Potential Partner List: Adi—3/15
- *Key Result*: Sign 35 Tier 1 Partners: Adi—3/30
- *Key Result*: Secure 500k Partner ARR: Adi—3/30

OBJECTIVE TWO
Successful Acquisition Integration: Perry

- *Key Result*: Present Key Deliverables to Integration Product Roadmap: Mala—1/15
- *Key Result*: Achieve Cross-sell Revenue Acquisition Targets with Existing Accounts: Adi—1/15
- *Key Result*: Complete Operations Integrations Top 10 List: Skyler—3/30
- *Key Result*: Complete Post Merger Financial Integration: Whitney—3/30

OBJECTIVE THREE
Complete Functional Process Maps: Skyler

- *Key Result*: Gather and Present Cross-functional Requirements from Each Functional Team: Skyler—1/15
- *Key Result*: Receive Functional v1 Process Map From Each Team for Review: Perry—3/15
- *Key Result*: Present and Distribute Process Map Digital Book: Skyler—3/30

OBJECTIVE FOUR
Set the Stage for Gartner Visionary Status: Stephen

- *Key Result*: Prioritize Industry Playbook AI Development Capabilities: Mala—2/10
- *Key Result*: Increase G2 Rating from 4.5 to 4.7: Nikolay—1/15
- *Key Result*: 3 Successful Analysts Interviews: Mala—3/15
- *Key Result*: 7 Product Feature Media Mentions: Stephen— 3/30

OBJECTIVE FIVE
Stand Up Data and Analytics Teams

- *Key Result*: Define, Present and Approve Hiring Plan: Julia—1/10
- *Key Result*: Define and Present Data and Analytics Roadmap and Stakeholders: Julia—2/30
- *Key Result*: Present Approved Budget of Data Infrastructure and Tools: Whitney—3/15
- *Key Result*: Approved Data and Analytics Roadmap: Julia—3/15

FUNCTIONAL OBJECTIVES: LATE STAGE

Corp and Cap Dev Objectives

- Provide Data Room Assets: Aiden—1/10
- 12 Strategic Investor Meetings: Perry—3/15
- Three Tier One Client Visits: Perry—3/15
- Complete Leadership Team Talent Mapping: Aiden—3/28

Biz Ops Objectives

- Complete and Present 2023 Operations Plan: Skylar—1/20
- Schedule Meeting Cadences Across Company: Skylar—2/28
- Data Room Complete: Skylar—3/20

Sales Objectives

- Achieve Rolling 10.m ARR: Adi—3/31
- 35 Fortune 500 Meetings: Adi—2/15
- Select and Secure Budget for Sales CRM Tool: Nia—2/15
- Hire 2 Business Development Reps: Adi—2/28

Marketing Objectives

- Reach > 3:1 LTV:CAC Ratio: Stephen—3/31
- Secure 35 MQLs: Luka—3/31
- Develop Three Marketing Campaigns and Launch One: Luka—3/31
- Define Requirements for Marketo Implementation: Stephen—3/31

Product Objectives

- Attain < 85% Weekly Product Feature Usage: Mala—3/31
- Update Customer Analytics Requirements: Mala—1/31
- Complete Updated Industry Playbook AI Development Capabilities: Zara—1/30
- Present Product Feature Scoring System: Mala—2/30

Engineering Objectives

- Release Customer Analytics Module: Julia—3/15
- Complete Testing on CAM: Nguyen—3/05
- Submit Training Developer Training Requests: Nguyen—2/28
- Hire Data Security Consultant and Manage SOW to Completion: Julia—3/10
- Define Upgrades for Outsourced Internal IT Plan: Julia—3/10

Customer Success Objectives

- Secure > 68 NPS: Nikolay—2/15
- Realize Churn Rate < 0.07: Rosa— 3/15
- Secure Top Three CX Platform Proposals: Leila—2/15
- Select CX Platform: Leila—3/10
- Launch Customer Jam Campaign: Rosa—1/15
- Define and Document New Onboarding Process: Nikolay—2/15

Finance Objectives

- Maintain > 20 Month Runway: Whitney—2/15
- Define and Document Budgeting Process: Whitney—2/15
- Define Scorecard for Corporate Controller and Launch Search: Whitney—3/1

People Objectives

- Earn > 8.1 Employee Health Score: Jax—2/15
- Update Company Hiring Plan: Jax—1/15
- Define and Document Recruiting Process: Jax—2/15
- Define and Document Employee Scorecarding and Review Process: Jax—2/15

TEAM KPIs: EARLY STAGE

Annual Metrics	Owner	Quarter 1	Quarter 2	Quarter 3	Quarter 4
650k ARR	Arianna	240k ARR	360k ARR	500k ARR	650k ARR
2.1m Seed Round	Arianna	250k	2.1m	2.1m	2.1m
3 Product Releases	Carlos	1 Product Release	0 Product Release	1 Product Release	1 Product Release
< 0.06 Churn Rate	Alex	< 0.10	< 0.09	< 0.07	< 0.06
Monthly Active Users	Sophia	85	90	100	120

TEAM KPIs: LATE STAGE

Annual Metrics	Owner	Quarter 1	Quarter 2	Quarter 3	Quarter 4
46m Series B	Perry	0m	20m	46m	46m
10% Operational Efficiency	Skyler	0%	3%	8%	10%
15m ARR	Adi	10.2m	11m	13m	15m
> 3:1 LTV:CAC Ratio	Stephen	> 2.3:1	> 2.6:1	> 2.8:1	> 3:1
< 95% Weekly Product Feature Usage	Mala	< 85%	< 88%	< 92%	< 95%
6 Product Releases	Julia	1	3	5	6
> 70 NPS	Nikolay	> 68	> 69	> 70	> 70
> 20 Monthly Runway	Whitney	> 20	> 20	> 20	> 20
> 8.8 Employee Health Score	Jax	> 8.1	> 8.2	> 8.6	> 8.8

EIGHT

TAKING BACK CONTROL

"The goal is to turn data into information,
and information into insight."

–CARLY FIORINA

" T'S A TOTALLY DIFFERENT FEELING NOW. I FEEL LIKE WE actually have control of the company again."

I was checking in over a video call with the CEO of the EdTech Company I'd worked with in New York two months prior, and I could tell from the energy he was bringing that the situation had completely turned around.

"Everyone's clear on what's most important, and what we need to work on first. And because we have so much focus and clarity, we're seeing results we can really be proud of. Peak gave us back the rudder, and put the wind in our sails."

His face, even over the video call, looked visibly less stressed. It's an effect I've seen in almost every team I've worked with: once the team starts clicking together and working in symbiosis, the CEO doesn't have to spend all their time answering questions and making team-level decisions that should really be owned by other leaders in the company. Without symbiosis, everything tends to trickle up to the CEO because no one is entirely sure what they're supposed to be aiming for. With Peak OKRs and KPIs, the team has a map of not just *what* they're supposed to do, *how* they're supposed to do it, and *who* is owning it, but also what their results will look like—in the form of visible, trackable metrics. Time, capital, and energy are all maximized.

"That's great. I'm happy to hear the team is leaning into it," I said. "How's the raise going?" I wanted to see if the team's newfound symbiosis was creating the results they needed.

"It's back to smooth sailing," he said, excitement obvious in his words. "It's going faster than I'd even hoped. It helps that our Board now knows exactly what we're aiming at, and I'm going into meetings with them with actual results to show, rather than what I used to do, which was prep a whole speech about why we couldn't hit our targets."

He continued to describe the changes in the team for a solid twenty minutes, and I just let him talk—when things start feeling good, and when things get done, the excitement is real!

"Providing this information to the board has also been really helpful for me. My independent board director was able to provide some insight from past experiences that were similar to our situation that probably would not have occurred to him if I was sharing what I used to share in board meetings."

"The endless grind feeling is gone. It feels great to see results, and it's way more fun when we're getting them together. Our energy is up and we're motivated. Getting wins together constantly is creating the most intense momentum, and everyone feels it."

"The KPIs we set are totally helping us learn the business better—you were right on with that. Every time we review KPIs we get better at predicting what's going to happen and projecting better targets. It's starting to feel like we're building a magic 8 ball. And the team gets it, too. We know we might miss some targets, but our intent in setting them is to learn, and that changes the mindset to winning."

"The speed and direction of the company don't feel out of control anymore. We know exactly where we're headed and we're all grounded in the pace we're setting. The functional areas are actually moving down the field *together* instead of an all-out sprint with people scattered all over. And for the first time, it feels like we have control of the levers."

It's always fun to catch up after sessions and feel the energy the CEO gets when their team truly comes together. I was thrilled for him, and excited to have another Peak Team in the Collective Genius community.

Back to our habit loops: the excitement of wins is the reward that helps cement the habits. With more wins, the team leans further and further in, getting better at the Peak habits and tools and creating even more wins.

CASE STUDY: EMPLIFY

I conducted this interview with Adam Weber, Co-Founder of Emplify

When the Emplify team began working with Peak, nearly all of us had already experienced various versions and philosophies of OKRs. What often hindered us was that at tech companies, everyone comes with their version of an OKR, leading to a slow decision-making process. Some teams used the 70% rule, some used the 100% rule, some viewed OKRs as milestones, and others saw them as metrics. The moment that truly stood out to me with Peak was the sheer simplicity of creating an objective. The question was direct: "What are we trying to accomplish?" It was a refreshing shift.

What I noticed was that when teams only use key results as metrics, they often deviate from their plans in a matter of weeks. The inherent challenge is when you're pressured to hit overly ambitious targets. Goals are set too high, product release schedules are overly ambitious, and then teams have to grapple with the realization that their strategy might have been too ambitious from the start.

Peak had an interesting approach to tackling this. In our Launch session, Jeff emphasized reverse engineering. Starting with a broad three-year vision, the team would align to that, then break it down into a one-year plan, and then into a 90-day plan. This process involves determining the most important objectives and key results as a team. Everyone contributes, everyone listens, and everyone participates in refining the objectives to the most important ones we need to knock out.

I was genuinely bought into the system, having already taken in all the tutorials on Peak OS Access. The team got bought in quickly as well, I think mostly because Peak wasn't a drastic departure from our previous approach—it was more like a refined version that resolved some of our earlier stumbling blocks.

I could feel a distinct turning point in our team immediately after our first Camp meeting. It was probably the best internal meeting we'd ever had. It wasn't just about the positivity, but the efficiency as well. We discussed several blockers in that meeting, which typically would dominate an entire meeting; this time, we effectively listed out our challenges and focused on the most important discussions. This not only saved time but also created a momentum where we were making decisions and executing them one after the other. It felt like a debt snowball payoff—we were continuously achieving small wins.

Attending these meetings meant something was going to get resolved. It wasn't just about listening and leaving. We adjusted our plans swiftly and saw a surge in our team's pace. It felt like everyone was more alert, knowing they'd be accountable every week instead of waiting until the end of a project.

Around the time we were implementing these changes, the backdrop was the COVID-19 pandemic. We had just reduced our team size by 20%. While this was initially hard, the situation turned into an opportunity. With a leaner team composed of our top talent, our productivity soared. We moved from a two-year stagnant phase to a growing trajectory. That momentum and renewed energy led us to a successful business exit.

PART 4

COMMUNICATION

NINE

WHEN TALKING ABOUT WORK ISN'T WORKING

"The single biggest problem in communication
is the illusion that it has taken place."
—GEORGE BERNARD SHAW

" I'M GLAD YOU'RE HERE—I NEED YOUR HELP."

It was a Peak CEO I'd worked with a few years back; I'd just wrapped a session teaching Peak tools to a group of founders. I'd been invited down to a VC founders retreat in Puerto Rico by one of our Collective Genius venture partners to run a session on the core habits and Peak. I enjoy going to these events. As a founder myself, I've always just naturally aligned with founders; the energy, passion, and purpose just connect with me. Plus, what I give in these sessions always seems to come back around.

This particular CEO had brought me in to work with his company every quarter for a year and a half, up until they successfully raised their Series B round. This is similar to most Peak teams—I'll do a year or two of Peak Sessions until they've got it down, and then they'll use Peak OS Access to train an internal team member to take over as Guide. (Note: Most Peak Teams are subscribed to Peak OS Access, which acts as a digital resource and guide no matter where they are in the process.)

The CEO fell into step beside me as we made our way out of the workshop room and out toward the bar, where everyone was congregating for happy hour.

"A few of the things you talked about in that session just now really connected. I feel like the team is still doing great with most aspects of Peak... except something is off in our meetings."

"What would you say feels off?" I asked.

He sighed. "Where do I begin?" Then he laid it all out on the table as we waited for the bartender to make our drinks.

"Meetings are endless. We have way too many. It's become a joke—anytime anyone has the slightest problem, or a new idea, we schedule a meeting."

"In meetings, I feel like we're talking about the same things over and over again. Sometimes it almost feels like we made

WHEN TALKING ABOUT WORK ISN'T WORKING

progress—but then nothing comes of it. The next meeting, it's back to the same conversation."

"And when decisions actually get made, they seem to get lost. I find myself in another meeting and people start debating a subject we've already made a decision on. Issues never go away or get solved, no matter how many times we dissect them."

"Meetings usually start late. Then they run long. They're not focused. It feels like we jump around with no agenda, even when an agenda is set ahead of time—nobody sticks to it."

"We talk about doing the work so much that there's not enough time left to actually do it!"

"With all the time we spend sitting in meetings, you'd think we'd be solving all the world's problems in there."

The spicy margaritas—plus some chips and salsa—being set down in front of us snapped him out of his diatribe, which I actually regretted a little. He was doing a great job of letting me know exactly where I could step in and help the situation he was in.

"Let me ask you something," I said. "Are you still doing the Weekly Camp Meeting cadence?"

He shook his head. "We've kind of fallen out of practice with that one. We had a bunch of new team members join a year ago after Series B, and they had a few new ideas on how to stream-line the meetings. I thought I would give them some rope to show us their process, so the habit sort of...fell off."

It made total sense why his team was struggling to communicate effectively: the main Peak tools for practicing great communication, Triage and the Weekly Camp Meeting, weren't being utilized. In their place, the team was scrambling to fill the gap by throwing random bad meetings on the calendar.

They had no *system* for communication. Great communication doesn't happen on its own; it needs a framework and guidelines, and facilitation, just like anything else.

"So let me see if I've got this straight. "You guys found a way to have bad meetings—and decided to have a lot of them?" I paused, looking to see if he caught my half-joking summary.

He laughed. "Yes, we decided to try something new where we'd fix our bad communication with more of it." We both laughed.

We hung out on the bar patio talking through the issue for another half hour, until our margaritas were empty and we had a plan of attack.

His team needed a refresher on Peak communication, and I had another trip on the calendar: heading out to his offices in Santa Cruz to guide them back on track.

TEN

A SYSTEM FOR COMMUNICATION

"Excellent communication doesn't just happen
naturally. It is a product of process, skill,
climate, relationship and hard work."

–PAT MCMILLAN

A S I WROTE EARLIER IN CHAPTER ONE, COMMUNICATION
is what brings teams together and keeps teams together.
It's the glue that holds an aligned, symbiotic team
together. Without great communication, it doesn't matter how dialed-in your 3YV, 1YP, OKRs, and KPIs are; getting

the work done requires effectively communicating across the entire team.

Poor communication in teams has been responsible for everything from failed businesses to blown sports games to aviation disasters. It creates an environment of confusion, conflict, and disengagement. It also makes building trust incredibly difficult; trust can only grow in an environment where everyone feels like they can say what they need to say, and be not only heard, but understood.

In *Outliers,* Malcolm Gladwell writes: "The kinds of errors that cause plane crashes are invariably errors of teamwork and communication. One pilot knows something important and somehow doesn't tell the other pilot. One pilot does something wrong, and the other pilot doesn't catch the error. A tricky situation needs to be resolved through a complex series of steps— and somehow the pilots fail to coordinate and miss one of them."

Venture-backed teams aren't flying planes, but the tricky high-wire act of doing something that's never been done before with huge financial stakes and a tight timeline for success is somewhat comparable. Building a successful VC-backed company requires building a team habit of excellent communication. So how do we do that?

Like all the habits I write about in this book, communication is something you can't leave to chance. Most people who make it to the level of skill and experience that gets them hired at a company like yours are likely pretty good communicators one-on-one. If they're in leadership, they're almost certainly good communicators when it comes to getting a message through to a group.

But team communication is different. It's not centered around one or two people. The entire group needs to cohesively communicate in a way that gets things done.

This leads to a primary complaint: *Nothing ever gets solved. We talk about the same problems over and over and they never get fixed.*

The solution to this problem is a Peak tool called Triage.

TRIAGE

Triage is one of the most important tools in Peak, and it never surprises me to hear from Peak teams that it's the most memorable part of the whole system. In fact, when I run into CEOs or team members years after working with them, I'll often hear something like, "We're still using Triage religiously!"

Triage allows a team to stay aligned, focused, and accountable. This is especially important to VC-backed teams, who are often pioneering new markets without a map. Problems and issues arise constantly, and there's no one who came before and left clues on how to solve them. There's no playbook to study. Without an effective way to prioritize, discuss, and solve problems, they'll quickly stack up and remain unsolved.

In its simplest form, Triage is a list of topics to be discussed. I like to say that Triage is the clearinghouse for making decisions. The items on the Triage List could be OKRs or KPIs that are off course; input or a discussion someone wants from the rest of the team; or action items that aren't going to get done on time. The things that go on the Triage List are things that require the team's collaboration to come up with not just *a* solution, but the *right* solution. The diverse minds in a team are always going to be better at fixing an issue for good than just one or two people.

The Triage List is a running list of issues, and sometimes opportunities, but it's important to differentiate it from a "parking lot". It's *not* a parking lot, for one key reason: the items on the Triage List aren't just going to sit there. They're going to get done.

Designated time for Triage is built into each Annual Session, Quarterly Session, and Weekly Camp Meeting (more in the next section). You'll never "skip" Triage; it's as much a part of any of these meetings as the agenda itself. With this habit built and reinforced every time you have a meeting, team members come to trust that the Triage List is taken seriously. They come to rely on Triage as the time when problems are solved together as a team.

At any point during the week, or during any meeting, any team member can add items to the Triage List. You can probably imagine the number of rabbit holes this habit saves the team from going down when someone brings up a new topic out of the blue. Instead of reactively jumping into discussion on every single new point that's raised, all you need to say is, "Great. Triage it." That team member does so happily, knowing that they can trust it'll be discussed at the designated time.

It's a little like the psychology behind a "cheat day" when you're on a diet. Designate Saturday as the day when you get to eat whatever you want, and it's a lot easier to say no to junk food on a Tuesday. You just put it on your wish list for your next cheat day, and your brain gets a little release valve from the craving. It'll be there waiting for you on Saturday! No need to keep thinking about it now.

Triage works the same way—it's a release valve for reactivity.

When it comes time to actually do Triage, it's not a simple rundown of the entire list that's accumulated in the Peak Team Dashboard. On the contrary, you're going to use a specific, repeatable process to work through your Triage List.

1. The meeting leader asks: "Is there anything on this list that's already done?" Typically, there are several items that actually "worked themselves out" since they were added to the list. Time tends to do that—another reason you want to avoid reactivity at all costs. A topic that arises Monday might not actually seem as urgent by Wednesday, and by Friday, it might have

been resolved or rendered irrelevant without the need to discuss it at all. Anything that's already solved gets removed from the Triage List.

2. Next, ask: "Is there anything we need to add to the list today?" Team members might speak up with new topics; add them to the Triage List. Anytime you add an item to Triage, put today's date next to it so you know when it was added.

3. Finally, it's time to decide what topics you're actually going to talk about *and solve* in this Triage session. You can't get through everything on the list, so you need to prioritize. And you don't want to just start at the top and work down—number 14 on the list might be far more urgent than number 10. Ask the team, "What are the most important and urgent items we want to talk about today?" Try to keep it to two or three items.

Once your Triage items for discussion are determined, it's time to ACT. On each item:

1. Assess the situation
2. Consider alternatives
3. Take action

I encourage the ACT habit in Peak because it drills exactly what you're there to do with Triage: take action. Get things done. Don't talk about doing them—*do them*. Don't put them off—do them now.

Let's say the Triage item being discussed is a software release. It's taking longer than the team working on it anticipated, and the head of engineering wants to move the release date back by a month. Here's how ACT would play out on that issue.

- **Assess the situation**: As a team, everyone thinks into the question, "What is the core issue?" Sometimes it needs to be asked multiple times, in multiple ways. The team might ask questions like, "Why are we doing more development?" or "What's taking so long with the development?" Without drilling down deeper, you may only solve symptoms rather than the root cause of the situation. Everyone in the room participates—just like at Peak Sessions, it's important for everyone to be involved in assessing the situation so you can be sure you've covered all the bases.

    While assessing the situation, it's uncovered that Engineering was given more requirements than were originally scoped. Aha—that's the core issue! That leads you to the next step.

- **Consider alternatives:** Here's where the team brainstorms all the different ways the problem could be solved—in this case, validating if it's worth it to try to meet the original deadline through other means. "What if we scaled back development? "Could we add more resources to the engineering team?" This step is where having a diverse group of people becomes a huge advantage. People who aren't subject matter experts tend to approach this brainstorm unfettered and unbiased, and will come up with alternatives that never would have occurred to the SMEs. I've seen engineers solve Finance problems, CFOs provide crucial input to product roadmaps, and more. What's most important is that the entire team puts their heads together and comes up with the widest range of alternatives possible.

- **Take action:** With all the options out on the table, it's time for the team to decide what they want to do. They'll decide on a course of action, and that action gets created as an item on the To Do List, with an associated owner and date. In this case, the team decides to pare back requirements so the engineering team can hit the original date. This is created as a concrete action: "Define new requirements." Actually defining the action is the step I so often see missed in meetings; a team will get all the way to the solution and then leave it there without defining *what* will happen next, *when*, and *who* owns it. For a Triage item to be solved, it has to have those questions clearly decided and communicated to everyone. Then, you add it to the team's To Do List in the Peak Team Dashboard.

And with that, you've knocked the item out! Move on to the next Triage item.

What happens if the team struggles to make a decision on the course of action to take? This is a huge indicator that there's not enough information to make the decision. Collecting that information would then be the next step action that lands on the To Do List. Either way, you're moving the ball forward and ensuring the problem will eventually be solved, even if it has to be pushed to the next meeting.

Your role as the CEO is critical during the decision making process. In fact, you're the linchpin to make sure decisions are *made*, not just talked about. If the team can't reach a consensus, and you have all the information needed—they just can't agree on action—then your job is to make the decision or empower someone else to do so.

Another hint on how to run great Triage: if there's nothing on the triage List, you're not going deep enough. But if you have too many items, ask the team: "How many of these are actually one-on-one conversations?" The likelihood is that a ton of items can be knocked off the list by resolving them outside the meeting with just a couple of people.

The habit your team is building in this process is not only great communication—by way of a system to collect, sort, prioritize, and discuss and solve problems—but also a bias toward action that is especially crucial for a constantly moving and adapting VC-backed team to master. There's no question of whether a Triage item is going to get done; there's no endless discussions that go nowhere. With ACT, the team is set up to *always* decide on a course forward and define clearly how it will be accomplished.

Your team also practices symbiosis here through the accomplishment of knocking items off the Triage List. Each item solved is a win; wins create momentum and shared accountability. The more items your team solves, the more work they can accomplish. It feels *great* to get things done instead of just talking about it. This emotional high is one of the reasons I hear Triage mentioned most often by Peak teams. They truly love it. It's simple, and it's a game changer.

WEEKLY CAMP MEETING

Patrick Lencioni, in *Death by Meeting*, emphasizes the significance of regular meetings, notably the weekly tactical meeting, for sustaining team alignment and accountability. He suggests that these sessions should focus on reviewing activities, addressing immediate issues, and synchronizing team efforts. This, Lencioni contends, ensures all team members are working towards a common goal. The accountability fostered in these meetings not only enhances operational efficiency, but also fosters an environment of shared understanding and progress. Meetings, as Lencioni sees them, are crucial for an aligned, focused, and accountable team.

I'll be diving into the entire rhythm of meeting cadences in Part Six: Learning. To start, let's break down the base unit of the Peak cadence: the Weekly Camp Meeting.

This is another "favorite part of Peak." If your team is plagued by meetings that are unproductive or that go too long, they're going to thank you for introducing the Weekly Camp Meeting.

This meeting is so powerful for building great communication because it follows a repeatable process that, once again, builds trust in the team. People trust that they will be heard, that all ideas will be considered, and that discussions will have structure and boundaries that enable things to get done, not just talked about.

The Weekly Camp Meeting is typically 60 to 90 minutes long, and it always starts right on time. Here's the agenda.

WEEKLY CAMP MEETING AGENDA

1. **Best and Thanks (5 minutes)**: We kick off with a quick charge of gratitude and positive energy. Everyone spends no more than one minute sharing their best personal or business experience over the past week, as well as one person they want to thank. This sets up the meeting for a positive, curious, open mindset.

2. **Peak OKR Review (5-10 minutes)**: In this section, you'll walk through OKRs—first the team OKRs and then the functional objectives. Each owner only responds with "On-Course" (meaning the OKR will be completed on time), "Off-Course" (it will not be completed on time), or "Done" (it's been completed). They can also respond "Push", meaning they're electing to stop working on the objective or key result for the remainder of the quarter. If they respond with "Off Course" or "Push", place the OKR on the Triage List for discussion.

3. **Peak KPI Review (5 minutes)**: In this section, you'll review your KPIs and define them as "On-Course" (the metric is reporting as planned) or "Off-Course" (the metric underperforming). All "Off Course" metrics are added to the Triage List for discussion.

4. **Team Updates (0-15 minutes):** The majority of the people in the meeting *do not* give updates. The rules for updates are as follows: Only the people who need to give an update will share one. Updates must apply to the majority of the people in the room, and updates must be prepared prior to the meeting. The update should not need a team discussion or decision. If a discussion or decision is needed, even a quick one, add it to the Triage List.

5. **To Do List (5 minutes):** First, walk through the list and remove any to-dos that have been completed. Throughout the meeting, you may add new to-dos, and if you do, add a name, owner, and the date it was added. The To-Do List helps the team stay on track and tracks the next steps from the Triage discussions.

6. **Triage List (35-45 minutes):** The Triage List is the most important part of the meeting. If you finish the first two or three items you designated, and you still have time in the meeting, select another two or three topics and repeat until you have 15 minutes left in the meeting. This habit is especially important because it will ensure that you always end the meeting right on time.

7. **Team Communication (5 minutes):** This section aims to share messages that can be passed down throughout the organization to those not in the meeting. This can be a message from anyone on the team to send through the organization.

8. **Rate and Close the Meeting (5 minutes):** The last step in the Weekly Camp Meeting is to rate the meeting. You'll do this to continually improve each meeting. Everyone will rate the meeting on a scale of one to ten—one being bad, ten being great. If anyone gives a rating under nine, they need to explain why. This learning step is critical for ensuring your Weekly Camp Meeting continues to become more effective for the team.

You'll use the Peak Team Dashboard to run this meeting; all the work you did in your sessions is centrally organized and accessible here, and it makes it easy for everyone to stay aligned.

The Weekly Camp Meeting is a powerhouse for building and reinforcing all the core team habits, not just Communication. Alignment and focus are created with the systematic review of OKRs, KPIs, and Triage items. Communication and transparency are fostered with the open, feedback-rich environment. Team members have a platform for sharing critical information, insights, and feedback that can improve operations and decision making. And for VC-backed teams, moving a million miles a minute and changing the game at every whistle, weekly meetings provide a regular touchpoint for leadership teams to review and adjust plans in response to new information, market changes, or unexpected events. This ensures that the team remains aligned, focused and adaptable, able to swiftly pivot or realign strategies as necessary.

Issues that plague a team and never get solved are like extra weight. The team will get dragged down the mountain if that weight keeps piling into their packs. Practicing great communication means that extra weight gets off their shoulders almost as soon as it lands, so they're only carrying issues a few feet before they're resolved.

At times, you're going to be off course; it's inevitable. However, it's better to be off course *together* than going in five different directions; at least when you're off course together, you can find your way back on course easier. This isn't a horror movie; we're not sending one person down into the dark basement to check on the weird noise. We're going to stay together as a team. Good communication is easy when everything's going great; it gets hard when things are challenging. Practice good communication now so that the team is always going to be able to move cohesively around whatever ravine stands between them and the top of the mountain.

EXAMPLES

TRIAGE LIST

Item	Name	Date
1. Rating system for product and feature development	Perry	3/12
2. Discuss pricing options for faster ramp expansion	Adi	3/12
3. Establish Solution Engineering Function	Julia	3/12
4. LTV:CAC Ratio > 5:1	Stephen	3/12
5. Hire CMO	Stephen	3/12
6. Identify Top 150 Strategic Accounts	Adi	3/12
7. Process hand off between marketing, sales and product	Perry	3/19
8. Secure Internal and External Product Council Members	Mala	3/19
9. Churn Rate < 0.06	Nikolay	3/19
10. International Expansion Options Discussion	Perry	3/19
11. Strategic Investor Decisions	Perry	3/19
12. New Office SF Space Survey Results Discussion	Whitney	3/19

ELEVEN

GETTING THINGS DONE

"When the trust account is high,
communication is easy, instant, and effective."
–STEPHEN R. COVEY

S ANTA CRUZ IS JUST A SHORT FLIGHT FROM WHERE I live, so when the CEO from the Puerto Rico retreat invited me out to his company's office, it was an easy trip. I ran a one-day refresher with his team on Triage and The Weekly Camp Meeting.

Listening to the team talk, it was clear that the CEO wasn't the only one fed up with the number of meetings on their schedule. The Head of Engineering was especially vocal: "I'd rather have *zero* meetings than the dozens we currently have clogging up our calendars," he said dramatically.

"Yeah, but you'd rather have zero meetings no matter what," the CEO joked, and everyone, including the Head of Engineering, laughed.

"See, you get me!" he replied. "But seriously, there has to be a way we can solve problems as a team and still have time and space to actually get things done."

I realized that the Head of Engineering hadn't been with the company back when we originally worked together. The same was true of easily half the room; as the CEO had described, much of the team were new faces.

"Well, that's exactly what I'm going to share today," I said. "Those of you who were here two years ago: who remembers Triage?"

A few people raised their hands. "Yes! That was that process that helped us be more productive," one longer-term team member said.

I was definitely glad to hear the Peak tools had stuck in their memory. (What would have been even better was if they never stopped using them in the first place, but hey, I get it; VC-backed companies change every five minutes.) We got to work breaking down and practicing Triage, and by the end of the session, the team was all in and ready to get back to the more structured, productive Weekly Camp Meetings they'd had in the past.

After the session, back home, I attended and guided their first Weekly Camp Meeting via video call. Then it was time once again for them to go out on their own. I received a calendar invite to guide their next Quarterly Session to see in person how the team was doing.

Walking around their beautiful, spacious offices near the beach, it sure seemed like they were back to chugging along with no major interruption to their growth. The energy was happy, productive, and as relaxed as is possible in a company at their stage (where a certain amount of manic energy tends to exist no matter how Zen everyone is).

The CEO filled me in on how the Weekly Camp Meetings had been going. "It's amazing. Meetings feel like they actually have *intent* now. We're not meeting just to talk about things, and we're not reflexively opening up discussions on items the moment they appear. Having that Triage List is a huge game changer."

We took a seat on a couple of easy chairs in their lounge, and the CEO cracked open a bottle of Pellegrino for us, mirroring our earlier Puerto Rico heart-to-heart over top-shelf tequila. "At the first one we did on our own a couple weeks ago, without you there, I was a little worried initially. But now the team seems to be getting better and better at Triaging each meeting. I'm also getting better at empowering them to make decisions."

"Great. That sounds like you're making forward progress."

He nodded. "The best part," he continued, "is that team members actually *look forward* to Camp. They know they're going to get that hit of knocking out Triage items, and they know the rest of their week isn't going to be taken up with random, reactive discussions to things that might not even be full-fledged issues. Remember our Head of Engineering saying that he wanted zero meetings?"

I nodded. "Yes, of course."

"Well, he came into my office the other day and told me, 'The Weekly Camp Meeting is the best part of my week—one meeting to rule them all.' He said he's going to implement it with his Engineering team, too."

I thought that would happen, I said to myself. "It probably helps that his calendar is now clear to just knock out his objectives rather than talking about them," I said, and the CEO laughed.

"Exactly!" he agreed. "We all got our calendars back."

CASE STUDY: FLOWSPACE

I conducted this interview with Anne Hallock,
the Chief Revenue Officer of Flowspace

When I joined the company, Flowspace hadn't yet fully formalized a remote-first model, but the pandemic really pushed us into that change. We had clusters of employees around Cincinnati, home to our engineering office and our CTO, and a business-focused team in Los Angeles.

Each location had its unique culture.

With the move to remote work, we needed to find ways to create connection and clarity within our teams. We looked to companies like GitLab for inspiration and began to emphasize asynchronous work, auditing meetings, robust documentation, and clear communication.

Working with Peak helped level us up even more when it came to communication, and the system was absolutely pivotal to the company's transformation into a remote-first culture. Peak provided a transparent overview of the company's priorities, ensuring everyone was on the same page. And we hadn't been on the same page, as we discovered.

When we began with Peak, we noticed some major misalignments right away; for instance, our sales and customer success teams measured a shared metric differently, which was leading to discrepancies in understanding whether it had been achieved. Peak helped us recognize and fix this.

For the first time, we understood how to build unified goals.

Triage has completely changed how we work. Anyone can bring up anything they're worried about, and they know it will get discussed and solved. Before, some people would try to pull strings behind the scenes, like going straight to the boss—but now, with everyone having a say, those tactics don't work.

The impact of Peak isn't just our systems and meetings. It's about how we talk to each other every day. The culture throughout the team is much more oriented to finding solutions than just chatting about problems.

When I first started here, my inbox was flooded with long email chains that just went on and on. It was crazy trying to keep up! But those are gone, and we're all working off the same page now.

Even outside of work in more casual settings, if someone mentions a work-related issue, we'll say "Triage it." It's been built into our vocabulary.

Recently, we were collaborating with a partner capable of doubling our business in the next 18 months. Initially, it was just a project under one team, but Peak helped us realize it deserved top priority, bringing together engineering, product management, and operations. Now, it's a collective effort with a ton of collaboration.

Our business has really changed for the better since starting Peak, and if I had to pick one word to describe it, I'd say "momentum."

Before, we were challenged to communicate effectively across time zones, geographies, and teams. Peak helped us find a clear direction and stay aligned.

Before Peak, everyone viewed their roles through their respective lenses, but now it's more unified.

Our company's main goals and direction are also much clearer. Peak has given us a shared language, and it's made it easier for the whole team to understand each other and connect more efficiently and effectively.

PART 5

EMPOWERMENT

TWELVE

WHEN YOU'RE IN YOUR OWN WAY

"In diversity there is beauty and strength."

—MAYA ANGELOU

ESSIONS IN AUSTIN, TEXAS ARE AMONG MY FAVORITE, because it means I'm going to get to eat Texas barbeque. One of my friends is the CEO of a Series B HealthTech company there, so when I landed in Austin the day before their Peak Teams Launch Session, I was thrilled to get a simple text from her: a pin dropped on a barbeque joint.

Hungry?

Yes. I was. I grabbed an Uber from the airport, and soon enough found myself seated at a rustic picnic table outside a yellow trailer with MICKLETHWAIT hand-painted across its metal side.

I've had barbeque enough times to know that if you're eating brisket off of paper plates outside in the sweltering heat, preferably on a random patch of grass and dirt that has a smoker and a food truck parked on it, it's going to be *really* good.

This was no exception. "This place isn't as famous as the big boys, but it's right up there with them in terms of quality," my CEO friend said as I savored the unbelievable food.

Next to her sat her co-founder, who also held the role of Head of Sales for the company. It was the first time we'd all spent time together.

"So, what are you most hoping to get out of the session tomorrow?" I asked the CEO.

"Honestly, if I walk out of there with everyone still on the team, it will be a miracle."

I almost choked. "Wait, what? What's up?" I hadn't heard anything like this from her in the run up to the session.

She sighed. "I'm struggling to get any of these people to stand up and lead. They're all in senior leadership, and I can't get them to actually *own* anything."

Continuing, she told me that team members weren't rising to the challenge of hitting specific sales metrics for their upcoming fundraising. They were having enough success to raise a Series C, but they weren't gaining enough momentum to raise at the valuation they felt they warranted and deserved.

"Some of them are so reluctant to make decisions, it feels like the whole company is walking through waist-high mud. We're hitting our targets, but barely. When a member of our board suggested we work with you on Peak, I jumped at the chance. I can't believe I didn't think to ask you before this, actually. I've been at my wits' end for months."

"Is it a people issue, or a process issue?" I asked.

She shook her head. "I'm not sure. If it *is* a people issue, it would look really bad if I fired the entire leadership team after selling the Board on how great they are. And if it's a process issue, then what does that say about me as a CEO, and my ability to operate the company?"

I asked her: "What happens when you try to get them to make decisions?"

She gave me the full rundown, and I took mental notes as she talked.

"We hired great people, but they always need our feedback before moving a single inch. They refuse to make decisions without me or our co-founder getting involved."

"It's not clear to them who owns what and who's supposed to be making decisions on certain things, no matter how many times we've been over it. Nobody wants to 'step on anyone's toes', so they're not stepping anywhere at all."

"Even our rockstar employees won't make a move without checking with me or our co-founder first. The bad habit has trickled down to the good people, too."

"Then, recently, one of the few people on our leadership team that didn't need handholding left for another company. I was absolutely shocked and heartbroken. Why did he have to leave, when all these other people who are my problem are still here?"

She rounded off her download with a statement that made me wince: "Call me an evil dictator, but if I just need to tell everyone exactly what to do, then that's what I'm going to do. I can't keep waiting for them to figure it out."

Well. Tomorrow's session was going to be interesting.

From what she described, I knew two things: one, that their problem would only get worse unless it was addressed quickly and they committed to Peak; and two, that these were common signs that there might be a problem with people, roles, or both. I was looking forward to helping solve this with them in the session.

The next day, we drove out to Wimberley and stayed at a beautiful ranch resort, with quaint cabins and a large central lodge where we held our session. The lodge was catered with snacks and drinks, the room had floor-to-ceiling windows that filled the room with cheerful Texas sunshine, and the team? Well, it was a mixed bag.

I've worked with hundreds of teams, and over the years, I've developed a pretty good radar for sensing when some people in the room are uncomfortable. That day, there were a variety of attitudes present. Some of them were excited. Some were nervous. Some looked skeptical. And a few of them probably needed a second cup of coffee.

I kicked off by reminding them that we were all in this together for the good of the company.

"And what's good for the company is good for all of us, by extension," I said. "A rising tide lifts all boats."

Some of the discomfort I sensed eased up a little bit, but it was still there.

"Let me also say that in this room, we're going to dig deep. We're going to call out the elephants in the room. We have to get up a mountain together, and you've been carrying these elephants for too many miles!" Scattered laughter, and finally, most of them were smiling.

After guiding the team through the morning session, and observing their dynamic together, it was clearer to me what was really going on with them. The CEO had been partially right: the team did struggle to take ownership, and looked to her for hand-holding on every tiny decision. But it wasn't because they were all bad fits. In fact, most of them were great and had a ton of potential.

I'd never lay the entire problem at the feet of a single person, but as CEO, in the big chair, sometimes you have to take a bigger share of the responsibility. And that was clear here: one big piece of the puzzle was the CEO's unwillingness to step back and *let* her team make decisions. In the Team Surveys, the team spoke of feeling scrutinized and micromanaged. Having been told through this behavior that they needed constant supervision, even the good leaders in the room felt totally disempowered. They didn't want to make a single move without getting approval, because the CEO's *dis*approval was so frequent.

Another huge drag on momentum was split decision-making ownership between the two co-founders, the CEO and Head of Sales. This came out in the Team Surveys as well. In discussion, the picture became even clearer.

"It feels like I need to take everything to *both* co-founders to get a decision made."

"Sometimes they're not on the same page, so I'll get conflicting instructions."

"Every time I want to make a move, I have to pitch it to both of them. The time I spend selling what I'm doing to them is time I could be spending actually getting it done."

At its heart, this was a people issue. This team needed to get clear on what their roles were, what they owned, and what they were responsible for, quickly. And the CEO and Head of Sales, the two co-founders, needed to acknowledge that they had accidentally created an environment where everyone was walking on eggshells.

Luckily, the next part of the session was what was going to clear up ninety-nine percent of the problem: Peak exercises called Roles & Responsibilities and Talent Mapping.

THIRTEEN

RIGHT PEOPLE, RIGHT ROLES

"A band is like an organism. It grows and changes.
It's never exactly the same. You bring in new
people, and they bring in new influences."

—FLEA (RED HOT CHILI PEPPERS)

WHEN A TEAM IS FULL OF SMART, TALENTED, EXPERI-
enced, skilled people, and none of them are stepping
up to take ownership of what you *know* they're capable
of, you're almost certainly dealing with an Empowerment problem.

You're probably dealing with other issues, too, but Empowerment is the core behavior that's not happening, and the behavior that needs to be instilled and practiced for the team to move forward.

In a team that doesn't feel empowered—or worse, as in the case of the Austin team, feels *disempowered*—engagement and productivity go out the window. After all, why care about your work when someone else is blocking your responsibility for it? Why work hard when you have no say in your work? Why take pride in your role when you're not sure what your role really encompasses?

Employees who aren't empowered don't believe that the work they do will make a difference. They're accustomed to having decisions made for them, or, when they do make those decisions, having those decisions overridden. They don't feel ownership over the work they do, because they've been shown that, at the end of the day, they *don't* own it. They don't feel heard or that their opinion matters in the grand scheme of things. They go through the motions. Morale plummets, and with it, productivity and performance.

The feeling of constantly being micromanaged, or that work is being overly scrutinized, is another empowerment killer. It creates a paranoid Big Brother-esque environment for *everyone*, so no one wants to make a move without getting it cleared first. This team felt frustrated and demotivated—ironic, since that's exactly what the CEO was feeling as a result of the situation, too.

Finally, when team members are not empowered, they may be less likely to make decisions or take action on their own. This can lead to delays, missed opportunities, and poor decision-making, which severely impacts not only the team's goals, but the company's as well. In VC-backed companies, forward momentum is *everything*. It's almost always better to take action, even at the expense of a wrong decision. Anything that stalls progress needs to be rooted out and eliminated quickly.

Across the hundreds of VC-backed companies I've worked with, I've never seen a successful one that didn't show consistent empowered behavior across all team members. Empowerment is truly the dealbreaker for VC-backed company success, and if you're seeing signs that your team lacks empowerment, you found this book just in time.

As Patrick Lencioni, author of *The Five Dysfunctions of a Team*, writes: "Organizational clarity allows a company to delegate more effectively and *empower* its employees with a true sense of confidence."

Successful VC-backed teams empower their members, providing autonomy and support for decision-making and ownership of work. When people have autonomy, they are more engaged, more creative, more motivated, and ultimately, more productive. Empowerment promotes the following:

- **Motivation:** Empowerment is a key factor in motivating team members to perform at their best. Having a strong sense of ownership over your work creates a deeper motivation to succeed at it.

- **Creativity and Innovation:** Empowered team members are more likely to take risks, generate new ideas, and think outside the box. This can lead to greater creativity and innovation within the team, which is essential for staying competitive, especially at the high-stakes levels of VC-backed companies.

- **Flexibility and Agility:** Empowerment allows team members to be more flexible and agile in their work. Team members have the freedom to make decisions and take action without constantly seeking approval from superiors, they can respond more quickly to changing circumstances, and they make better decisions.

Peak builds empowerment in teams in a couple of key ways:

- **Roles & Responsibilities:** In Peak, defining and sharing roles and responsibilities is a core element in building a high-performing cross-functional team. Roles and responsibilities refer to the specific tasks and duties assigned to each team member, outlining their areas of accountability, decision-making authority, and collaboration strategies for achieving team goals. VC-backed teams are growing and changing so quickly that it's even more important that this is part of the cadence.

- **Talent Mapping**: As your organization evolves, so will the structure of the team needed to reach your destination. This tool helps you re-map your team on an annual basis to ensure you have the right people in the right roles, or as Jim Collins writes in *Good to Great*, "the right people in the right seats".

ROLES & RESPONSIBILITIES

In his book *The 17 Indisputable Laws of Teamwork*, John C. Maxwell discusses the importance of finding the right person for the right position within a team. He writes, "The Law of the Niche says that all players have a place where they add the most value. Essentially, when the right player is in the right place, everyone benefits."

You can't leave this up to chance, nor can you hire great people and just hope for the best. In my experience, it's *especially important* in teams of highly talented, top-of-their-field

A-players to clearly and carefully define who exactly owns what so that everyone can operate with autonomy and trust.

Having clear roles and responsibilities ensures team members have a common understanding of their tasks, responsibilities, and expected outcomes. It reduces confusion, makes sure there are no duplicated efforts, and eliminates conflicts over decision-making and ownership. Each functional area owner needs to have absolute clarity on what they need to do and how it ties into all the other functional areas; once they do, they're free to run, unrestrained.

Where many companies go wrong with this is just drawing up an org chart and calling it a day. Teams are living, breathing units; and with change as constant as it is in VC-backed companies, the roles and responsibilities of individuals—and the talent needs of the team—tend to change as well. Peak allows for not only the definition of empowerment, but the *practice* of it, by making Roles & Responsibilities a regular exercise in the meeting cadence. Making it a habit to review R&R, and not leaving it to assumption, allows teams to identify any gaps or overlaps in their capabilities, ensuring that each team member's strengths and areas for improvement are leveraged effectively. It also provides a critical opportunity for teams to reflect on their overall performance and identify areas for improvement.

Annually, during the Peak Annual Session, the team's roles and responsibilities are redeveloped in pre-planning and reviewed during the session. The Roles and Responsibilities tool, like all Peak cadences and tools, can be utilized by every team in the organization.

In the prep work for the Annual Session, team members are asked to define the following for themselves:

1. Title
2. Functional Area
3. Role
4. Top five responsibilities of that role

I typically guide the CEOs to be a part of this prep work with each individual. This ensures that when each team member presents their role at the Annual Session, everything is already aligned, and we're not losing time to any clarification that could have been hashed out ahead of time.

Then, in the session, prior to creating the 3YV and 1YP, each team member presents their Role & Responsibilities. Each team member's R&R is mapped out and defined. Each team member verbalizes to the team what their responsibilities are, then walks through what they've identified as their five most important responsibilities.

At this point, I ask the group: "Any questions? Any clarification needed?"

We do this to absolutely ensure that everyone has a chance to get clear on who owns what. When a team struggles with ownership and empowerment, I'll hear things like, "I don't know who I'm supposed to go to for authorization/questions/ etc. I don't know who makes the final decision on that. I'm not sure where the boundaries are for what I can do on my own, and what's someone else's territory." Getting everything articulated verbally in the group, then getting all questions and confusion addressed when everyone is in the room together, goes a long way to ensuring clarity.

It's also a great opportunity for teams to discuss where they've had problems in the past. I've seen frequently that a CEO is unknowingly hamstringing their team by continuing to make too many decisions that should actually be owned by team members. The CEO sees it as team members not stepping up and owning their functional areas, but these team members often want nothing more than to make the decisions—they just need a definition of which ones are theirs to make. *With* that definition, however, they're free to take off running.

Being a longtime sports coach, I always think of this in terms of player positions on a team. If you've played baseball, you know how incredibly important it is that the third baseman doesn't suddenly decide to run out to the outfield to catch a pop fly. If you've played hockey, you know that the goalie's job is to stay in the box, and that leaving it to suddenly go play center would have disastrous consequences. And if you've never played a sport, you may have seen your sports-loving friends groan with frustration when a play falls apart in front of them—often due to players not being where they're supposed to be, not *playing their role*.

Whereas the incredible symphony created when each player on a team does exactly what they're supposed to do—which, not coincidentally, is what they're *most talented at*—is truly a sight to behold. It almost looks like the players are telepathic, so cleanly and efficiently does the ball move up the field toward the goal. Every player is in exactly the right spot, and every pass, throw, or move lands perfectly. It's amazing to watch, and it's what separates the champions from the rest of the pack.

This is exactly what happens in VC-backed teams when roles and responsibilities are clearly defined, articulated, and agreed upon. People feel a renewed energy and sense of excitement and purpose in their work. They know that they can be proud of the results they get. They also feel a new sense of respect for their teammates; they've been given a clear look at what everyone does, and can trust that the results they're not responsible for are safe in the hands of the other team members who own them.

TALENT MAPPING

This practice can work throughout the organization, but you'll start with the leadership team.

First, take a look at your most recent 3YV and 1YP. Thinking in terms of the year ahead, list your top five to ten functional areas that will be reporting to you, the CEO. Don't think in terms of who is currently on your team (the people), but only list the functional areas across a piece of paper horizontally—such as Sales, Product, Engineering, Finance, and others.

Under each function, define the roles and responsibilities of that function. Start by defining the objectives of the position over the next twelve months. This can easily be done by using your current 1YP that lays out each functional area objectives.

Next, list the additional responsibilities this functional leader will need to accomplish to be successful. For example, if they're leading and managing a team, you might define this responsibility as, "Manage a team of three product directors and one UX manager." Another responsibility could be working cross-functionally with other areas, or responsibilities supporting other functions in the organization.

Next, identify the skills and experience that would be ideal for this person to have to be successful in this position. Ask yourself, "What skills and experience would allow the person to accomplish their objectives and support them to be successful with their responsibilities?"

In the final section, simply list your organization's core values and create a section called "Motivation".

REVIEW THE TEAM

Now, with your team in mind, start matching your current leadership team to each of the functional areas one functional area at a time. Look at the objective, the responsibilities, and the ideal skills and experience. Is there an obvious fit with a current team member? Look at the core values. Do they clearly demonstrate and identify with these core values? Look at motivation. Are they motivated to do this role? Do they want this role?

As you evaluate the team looking across all the areas, find the gaps. Are there gaps in the functions compared to the person you see in the function? Are there gaps on the team where no one can fulfill that function?

DEFINE THE TEAM

Determine what gaps are manageable and reasonable. Define the areas you would like to grow your leaders and where you may need to hire or promote others. Best practices have shown that a functional team leader can be successful with some gaps in the skills and responsibilities if defined and empowered to develop. However, history has shown over and over that it's likely not a fit when there is a gap in either core values or motivation.

REFINE THE TEAM

Once you have made your decisions around your functional organization chart, find another one or two members on your team to share your findings. Work together to make final changes before sharing one-on-one with your leadership team members.

Schedule one-on-one meetings with each leadership member on your team. Review the organization chart and do a deep dive into their specific functional area. Share with them where you see a fit and where you see an opportunity to grow.

Ask each team member to take a week to review and make suggestions for changes within the Objectives, Responsibilities, and Skill & Experience. Ask them if they feel they match the core values and if they believe they're truly motivated to play this role in the organization.

In a follow up one-on-one meeting, review their potential changes and tweak as you see fit. If either you or they feel there's a gap in their skills and experience, ask them how you can help. Finally, discuss the core values and their motivation for the role.

This last step is critically important; it's entirely possible that someone fits the role(s), but either is not a fit culturally, or not motivated to *do* the role.

COMMUNICATE THE TEAM

With all the functional areas and leaders defined, schedule a time to have each leader share their function to the team. The best time to do this is in the Peak Annual Session. Knowing your role and others' roles will help everyone function better as a team.

STAYING EMPOWERED

In the future, when decisions arise that have unclear owner-ship, the team already has a tool that will help them quickly come to a resolution: Triage. To Triage this issue solves so many problems, and you'll find that ownership is often the root issue found in many Triage items. Triage it, and the area of ownership is quickly solved, the decision gets made, and the team keeps moving toward the goal.

Empowering the right people is the primary impact of R&R. But another key outcome is that the *wrong* people—those who aren't a fit, aren't performing, or aren't interested in being aligned with the rest of the company—are now seen via Talent Mapping. A clear map of what they're responsible for is on the wall (and in the Peak Team Dashboard for ongoing review). They're accountable to it. If they fail to achieve it, it's obvious, and the CEO's decision is made much simpler.

This doesn't always need to mean an exit. In fact, what sometimes seems like a wrong person is often actually just in the wrong seat, and getting clear on everyone's roles and responsibilities creates an opportunity to solve a problem the company has had for a long time.

PEAK TEAMS

EXAMPLES

ROLES & RESPONSIBILITIES

Name	Arianna
Title	Head of Sales
Role	Responsible for developing and executing the company's sales strategy, leading the sales team, and driving revenue growth to achieve the company's financial goals.
Responsibilities	• Develop and implement a scalable sales strategy that aligns with the company's business objectives and market opportunities. • Lead, manage, and coach the sales team to ensure they have the skills and resources needed to meet or exceed sales quotas. • Drive revenue growth by securing new accounts, growing existing accounts, and reducing customer churn. • Collaborate with other departments, like Marketing and Product, to align on go-to-market strategies, refine product offerings based on customer feedback, and ensure seamless customer experience.

174

TALENT MAPPING

Function	Sales
Three Year Vision	• 3.5m ARR • 50 Clients • Onboard Head of Sales and Scale Team
One Year Plan	• 650k ARR • Document Sales Methodology and Process • Implement Salesforce.com • Onboard Sales Executive and BDR • Develop 1,500 Prospective Companies List
Role	• Responsible for developing and executing the company's sales strategy, leading the sales team, and driving revenue growth to achieve the company's financial goals.
Responsibilities	• Develop and implement a scalable sales strategy that aligns with the company's business objectives and market opportunities. • Lead, manage, and coach the sales team to ensure they have the skills and resources needed to meet or exceed sales quotas. • Drive revenue growth by securing new accounts, growing existing accounts, and reducing customer churn. • Collaborate with other departments, like Marketing and Product, to align on go-to-market strategies, refine product offerings based on customer feedback, and ensure seamless customer experience.
Ideal Skills	• Relationship Building and Communication • Team Leadership and Management • Strategic Thinking and Planning • SaaS Product Knowledge • Sales Forecasting and Analytics • CRM and Technical Sales Proficiency

Ideal Experience	• Five years leading SaaS sales teams from 3m to 10m in sales growth • Three to five years creating GTM SaaS sales strategies • Experience in managing and cultivating relationships with clients • Experience in developing and implementing sales strategies in a SaaS environment • Experience working cross-functionally with marketing, product, engineering, customer success, finance, and people
Company Core Value	• Customer Obsession • Passion for Innovation • Focus on Operational Excellence • Be A Team Player • Results Oriented

Employee / Candidate	
Skills and Experience Gaps	1. 2. 3. 4. 5.
Core Value Gaps	1. 2. 3. 4. 5.
Alignment and Motivation Gaps	1. 2. 3. 4. 5.

FOURTEEN

MOTIVATED BY THE RIGHT ROLE

"A team is not a group of people who work together.
It is a group of people who trust each other."
–SIMON SINEK

COULD TELL HALFWAY THROUGH THE AFTERNOON SESSION
that the CEO was having an epiphany.

I always found her as one of the more aware founders I
know, so I wasn't surprised that it only took a couple of hours
and the presentation of each person's R&Rs for her to figure
out the key role she'd been playing in her own frustrations.

Because, as we got the R&Rs up on the session sheets and discussed each team member's unique role, design-making boundaries, and area of ownership, one thing became overwhelmingly clear: she had a great team of A-players who were more than capable of executing at the level of ownership she expected. They were just paralyzed by what felt like intense over-scrutiny of their work. They'd come into the company feeling sure of their decision-making, but one too many instances of the CEO herself stepping in to "help" had robbed them of that confidence. And the added feeling of needing to "pitch" their decisions to both co-founders—the CEO and the Head of Sales, who sometimes weren't even aligned—had led to a serious lack of engagement. This feedback was so unanimous throughout the rest of the team that the issue was added to the Triage List to be solved.

During a five-minute stretch-your-legs break, she pulled me aside. "Why didn't you just tell me I was contributing to the problem here?"

Even her question illuminated her mindset—*just tell people what to do, and they'll do it*. She may have started to understand where she'd been getting in the way, but the concept of ownership wasn't clicking all the way in quite yet.

"I'm just a guide in these sessions," I told her. "By allowing teams to find the solution together, they create ownership and buy-in much more than if you just tell them what to do. You and your team are doing a good job working this out together. Everyone's already a lot clearer on what they own and how to attack it."

She had to agree with that.

A half hour later, it came time for the Head of Sales (and co-founder) to review their R&Rs with the team. Within minutes, we had a heated conversation bouncing around the room.

"I know I'm supposed to hit the revenue numbers we've defined. But I'm not really seeing how we're going to do that, and it feels like my KPIs are built on a house of cards," he explained.

"But this has always been the goal," the CEO said. "We've never had a different expectation. Without those revenue targets being hit, we're not going to be able to continue to grow."

"I get that. I want the company to succeed as much as anyone. But I'm just not comfortable with a target I'm not sure I can hit."

The conversation was way off track; we were supposed to be talking about R&Rs, and somehow it had turned into a conversation about sales targets. I guided them back on track. "Let's add this topic to the Triage List. You guys will work on solving it in the next meeting."

After we completed the R&Rs part of the session, I asked both co-founders to step up and review the company's Mission Statement with the team. This is something we usually do first in a Peak session, but the team needed to see their two co-founders united on something.

It worked perfectly: CEO and Head of Sales were in lock-step, and clearly still incredibly inspired by the North Star they'd defined together when they'd started the company. As they talked through the Why, How, and Why+How of the team's mission, their infectious enthusiasm and passion for the mission came through like a wave of energy. The faces of their team members lit up as they reconnected with the mission. I could see exactly why such top players had been attracted to work with these co-founders in the first place; this was their wheelhouse. They knew exactly how to move a crowd, compel action toward a shared mission. It was inspiring to watch.

As the team broke for dinner later in the day, I could tell they were bouncing with energy. With everyone's owner-ship clearly defined, and with a reignited excitement in their mission, these top-level athletes could finally break loose and run down the field—something they'd been itching to do the whole time. I overheard eager conversations about the objectives they were going to go after first and how they were going to spark the same energy in their own functional area teams.

That's the thing about empowerment: it spreads like a wave. People *want* to take ownership, they *want* to make decisions, and above all, they want to succeed. Giving them clarity of their mission and responsibilities is like taking off a parking brake that had been keeping a sports car from getting up to speed.

Two weeks later, in a follow-up call with the CEO, the results of the R&Rs session spoke for themselves. "I feel like the team has been unlocked," she told me. "And without them coming to me or my co-founder every ten minutes for a decision, it's like I got my time back to focus on my own objectives. We've already got some quick wins under our belt, which is like fuel on the fire!"

"Speaking of your co-founder," I said, "have you tackled those Triage items yet?"

Not only had they tackled them, they'd crushed them.

The first big solution was hashing out the bifurcated authority problem. "We all agreed as a team that I'm the CEO, period. I'm the CEO for a reason. The final decision is mine, and if they need authorization for something that truly requires executive-level authority, then I'm the one they come to."

Perfect. That's exactly what the team needed.

The Head of Sales/co-founder's discomfort with sales targets was the next Triage issue they'd solved, and it had taken considerably more discussion—but the end result was actually a huge win for the entire company.

To solve it, the two co-founders had completed the Talent Mapping exercise to make sure they understood the evolved needs of the company. Once they had a clear picture in front of them of what roles the company needed most, it was clear that the Head of Sales was in the wrong seat.

As a co-founder of the company who happened to have a sales background, it had made sense when they started to have him own the Sales functional area. But in discussion of his R&Rs, it had become clear to both of them that the old saying "what got you here won't get you there" was at play. "He was the first to admit that not only did he not have the experience needed to take on these higher sales targets, he didn't truly have the motivation to do so, either. His biggest strength is in pitching, not grinding. He's charismatic and compelling in the room, but as an org leader, he doesn't have the experience— nor does he like doing it."

They had decided as a team to hire a CRO to build out and lead the sales organization, a decision that, once they came to it, seemed obvious and even overdue.

"Meanwhile, we placed him in a much better position: the new Head of Partnerships position that Talent Mapping helped us realize we needed. He's perfect for it, and it's much more aligned with his strengths and what he wants to be doing long term. He's already got a major partnership deal on the table and things are moving faster than ever—perfect timing, because we were starting to fall behind!"

The Talent Mapping exercise also uncovered some less-than-ideal fits with other team members. The CEO was able to put a plan in action to uplift their skill sets and experience to help them meet the needs of their roles—but with the clear understanding that if the gap continued, those team members might need to be replaced.

The part of this story that has always stuck with me, and that I hope sticks with you, is that the company's needs *have* to come first. Even someone as key to the company as a co-founder can lose their way, or not grow at the same speed as the rest of the organization. Talent Mapping helps define what the company truly needs most, and from there, the right role is either there, or it isn't. Don't be hesitant to make changes based on what the company needs.

With refreshed clarity around roles and ownership, the co-founder finding a better fit, and other team members progressing in their roles, the CEO felt a huge momentum gain. People were just happier, and happy people succeed—they know what they're responsible for, they can confidently get after it, and as a team, they celebrate far more wins.

An empowered team runs on clarity and trust: clarity in their roles and responsibilities, and trust that they'll be allowed to take off and run toward their results. Give them that, and you'll see them hit speed and momentum like you can't imagine.

CASE STUDY: SLINGSHOT AEROSPACE

*I conducted this interview with Melanie Stricklan
about her time as CEO and Co-Founder
of Slingshot Aerospace.*

Every startup needs focus. When you're just beginning, there are countless areas demanding attention: business operations, sales, marketing, finance, fundraising, and the intricacies of your business model, to name a few. Figuring out what you need to be driving toward and the priority level of each seemingly "top priority" item is harder than it sounds.

In the beginning, our startup felt divided, like two separate companies with distinct visions. My co-founders and I quickly understood that for us to continue gaining traction, we needed an unbiased expert trusted within the tech community to guide us and challenge our passionate opinions.

Initially, our success was gauged by our ability to secure funding and generate sufficient revenue for product development. However, our introduction to Peak and the subsequent team survey was a reality check. The feedback indicated a clear disconnect: our team wasn't aligned with the company's mission, core values, and vision. Their responses varied widely. This underscored an undeniable need for a fundamental change in our operational approach.

As a combat-tested USAF veterans, one of my co-founders and I were ingrained with the principle of defining the end goal upfront and relentlessly driving the mission towards that objective, all the while commanding decisively amidst chaos. Yet, amusingly, this discipline seemed to evade us in this new entrepreneurial journey. Diving into details, timelines, and the structural insights from Peak, it became glaringly obvious that Slingshot lacked mission and vision alignment. Our leadership team, though well-intentioned, was out of sync. The painful truth was, while we celebrated our revenue successes, we were inadvertently sowing discord within the company taking for granted that our team was focused on a single vision and mission.

Introducing Peak to the team introduced new friction—which had its own silver lining, in that it was immediately clear which team members were "on the bus" with the vision, and which ones weren't. As our sessions progressed, the friction always seemed to settle around two or three team members. This was tough, but it also drove a better understanding of how to interview, what to look for, and how to find the right talent. We realized we needed to find people who were eager to hang their ego at the door and work together in a team of teams led by a mission-driven perspective. To this day, actually, the mark of our work with Peak is all over the Slingshot hiring process—it made absolutely clear what kind of culture adds we're looking for. And internally, we became an engine of alignment and productivity.

The changes we made to the business weren't small. We dropped an entire half of the business's products and services, the "company #2" of the two-company business we realized we were operating. This was a huge shift, and we brought in PR experts to create a communication plan before pulling the plug. Throughout the change, we had the confidence of having not just identified but measured the friction that was happening; we knew the move we were making was the right one for our vision. We'd been making business decisions in a vacuum, driven by nothing more than who was giving us money. Now we were making decisions on a years-long roadmap that was solid and clear for the first time.

The work we did with Peak helped me understand not just myself as the leader of the company, but also helped me understand how to communicate with other points of friction in the company and operate better within that dynamic instead of just letting it fester and hoping it would work out. I came away with the ability to express the company's vision, mission, core values, north star, and waypoints. Once I was able to do that, I saw the team so much more clearly. Especially when it came to those who maybe weren't aligned, and maybe never had been. They could easily find alignment somewhere else, but that place wasn't necessarily Slingshot unless they were willing to hop on the same bus as the rest of us flying toward our North Star.

PART 6

LEARNING

FIFTEEN

WHEN YOU DRAW YOUR OWN MAP

"Alone we can do so little; together we can do so much."

–HELEN KELLER

THE LAST THING YOU WANT TO SEE WHEN YOU SWITCH your phone back from Airplane Mode after a bumpy landing is a deluge of panicked text messages from the very person you've traveled to meet with.

We just lost one of our biggest partners

Don't know if this is the right time to do a team session

Maybe when the dust settles in a few months? Hate to cancel, people have already traveled

Can you shoot me a message when you land? Thanks

I sent a quick reply that I'd call him in a minute, then gathered my things as I waited to deplane in Cancun. This Peak Annual Session had been planned during a company offsite retreat that had a good mix of recreation and work.

Mixed team offsite retreats are a frequent occurrence, and it's something I really encourage. Getting the team out of their usual office space and in a location where they're not having to worry about getting home in time for dinner tends to open people's minds and lead to deeper discussions. It's a shared experience that builds team unity. Plus, there's the incredible benefit of a team simply sharing "fun" time together and bonding. You don't often get to do that at home, beyond the occasional happy hour. Going all the way to Cancun isn't required, either—I've seen teams simply rent a coworking space in town, or borrow a conference room from a partner company. But the ideal is definitely getting completely away. I love a retreat out of state in the woods somewhere, or in a tropical location.

The Future of Work company I'd traveled to Mexico to work with was in their Series B. I'd worked with them for a couple of quarters, and then they ran Peak on their own for the next two quarters. However, in recent check-ins, I'd noticed a distinct drift away from the Peak framework and tools. This can happen after a team starts using the system; they are so used to change that they tend to believe change is always the answer. It's like they're on a new health regimen; at first, they're all charged up and eating perfectly and going to the gym every day, but at some point, they get stressed and knocked off their discipline. They skip the gym one day. The next day they go through their favorite fast food drive thru. From there: chaos. They're back to their old habits and behaviors.

This isn't how Peak works, though. It's built on the fundamentals, and its power is in its structure and consistency.

The CEO had suffered a quarter of missed targets, and had scheduled the Annual Session as an offsite retreat. The entire team would be arriving in Cancun that day to start the session the following morning.

And now the business gods had thrown the CEO a curveball, and he wanted to cancel—when getting back on track with Peak was the thing his team needed most.

As soon as I was off the plane, I popped in my AirPods and called the CEO as I walked to baggage claim. It connected immediately, with the CEO's voice saying a terse, "Hi Jeff." He sounded about as stressed as one would if they had a major company crisis on their hands.

"Hi. What's up?"

He explained the situation quickly, because there really wasn't much more to explain than what he'd texted me. Their biggest partner had parted ways, their revenue target for the rest of the quarter—frankly, the rest of the year—was in jeopardy, and he was in emergency mode trying to figure out what to do.

"I just think everyone needs to really lock down and focus on this problem, and I don't know that we'll be getting our best work done with this on all our minds," he told me.

I circled the baggage carousel. My luggage has duct tape all over it in an attempt to make it look beat up and undesirable; it's easy to spot. "How do you typically react to problems like this? Do you let the dust settle, or take action?"

"We typically group up, discuss the problem, and make a plan."

"Well, that's exactly why we're here. Let's get the team to lean into this offsite, do the important work of listening to each other, solving problems, and taking action—and spending time together celebrating the wins of this past year. You'll have time in the session to Triage and solve this problem. What better time is there than now, when you have the whole team together, ultra-focused and ready to act? They don't need to wait for dust to settle. We have the team together and focused—let's get on it."

My little speech wasn't just aimed at ensuring I wouldn't have to turn around and get back on the plane I'd rode in on. The CEO was truly missing the key to what makes Peak so powerful: consistency. It was where they'd gotten off track in the first place, and I could tell his mindset was still so focused on flexibility that he was underestimating the need for discipline.

For VC-backed teams, consistency is king. It's like quitting junk food: breaking consistency makes getting back on track even harder. What the CEO was doing now, in his panic, was the equivalent of buying a box of donuts and stress eating. It was only going to make things worse. If you want your team to be consistent, you need to be consistent.

By the time I was tossing my bags into my Uber, the CEO had changed his mindset. I could only hope that he'd show up the next day with his stress in check. No matter how understandable that stress might be, his team needed to see his buy-in and commitment to discipline.

The next day, the team arrived in the large resort lounge where we were holding the session fired up and ready to work. They'd been out late having fun the night before, and a few of them had even gotten up early to go for a beach run. The offsite was already working its magic: they were full out of the stresses of their "normal" home lives, and were more open-minded and ready to do some deep thinking.

We started off with a tool I use as the "cue" part of the cue > habit > reward sequence: "Best and Thanks". One by one, we went around talking about the best business or personal thing that happened in the last week, and one person they would like to thank. This cue denotes the start of the meeting, priming them for open, transparent, conversations that are focused on building together.

Next, we took a look at their Team Surveys.

"All right, what can you see in these?" I asked them.

One by one, team members piped up.

"Symbiosis is way better."

"I feel like Communication is up from last time—that's trending positive, right?" (It was.)

"We're still not great on Alignment."

"But we're better than last time! We did improve a little."

"Empowerment is better! Doing great there."

"Learning..."

I waited as they all looked over the surveys. Looking back on the surveys they'd also done previously, they could see that a lot had changed. As I suspected, Learning was where they were totally stalled, and I could guess why.

The CEO raised his hand. "Learning is dead in the water, if I'm reading this right."

"Well, I'd put it a little more positively than that," I said. "But yes, there's a big opportunity for improvement there. We can add it to the Triage list and dig into it today."

As we reviewed the survey, they shared a lot about how they were implementing (or not implementing) Peak.

- Over the past quarter they had slowly started running a "streamlined version" of Peak, due to, as they put it, being "too busy" for all of the discipline and tools they'd been doing. In case you were wondering—there is no "streamlined version" of Peak. It works via building habits, not avoiding the ones you don't want to make time for.

- Their Weekly Camp Meetings were, to put it lightly, a mess. They weren't following the framework at all. They never even got to Triage because they spent so much time giving updates and going off on tangents with the OKRs. They didn't use ACT, and issues didn't get solved. The one win was that they were, at least, meeting weekly.

- Scratch that. They weren't meeting weekly. They had been at first, and then they decided to switch to bi-weekly in Q4. I managed to swallow one of my old midwestern sayings: "Oh great, now what?"

- The team spoke up consistently about the OKRs not working well for them. This also came through clear as day on the surveys. Something hadn't clicked, and their OKRs were consistently being moved, redefined, or just left off.

Peak isn't just about meeting weekly and setting goals. The system is specifically designed based on the core habits and behaviors I identified in the top tier of successful VC-backed companies I've worked with throughout my career. Every tool, every habit, and the entire system holistically reinforces the habits that make teams win. In the words of the great Vince Lombardi, fundamentals win championships.

This wasn't the first time a team I worked with had decided to pick and choose the pieces they liked best and leave the rest. To date, it had never resulted in success, and this team was no different.

The core behavior they were stalled out on—Learning—is a direct reflection of the cadence and discipline of Peak. Without reinforcing the learning loops of the Weekly Camp agenda, the Triage system, ACT, and even the regular, reliable cadence, the team wasn't actually *building* their habits. They weren't learning through reinforcement.

We have a saying in Jiu Jitsu: *A black belt is a white belt that never quit.*

In other words: to truly become a master, you can never stop learning. You are always a white belt.

SIXTEEN

CONSISTENCY IS KING

"We are what we repeatedly do. Excellence,
then, is not an act, but a habit."

—ARISTOTLE

N VC-BACKED COMPANIES, THE ONLY CONSTANT IS CHANGE.
If a VC-backed team isn't practicing learning, becoming fluent
in the process of continual adaptation to new inputs, change
will be met with deep resistance.

Learning is a core behavior at the individual level and team
level. At the individual level, team members need to have a
learning mindset where they're always seeking growth, explor-
ing new ground, and reflecting on and assessing ground they've

already traversed. At the team level, the entire team needs to practice learning together, making continuous review and iteration a part of every objective they tackle together. Teams not willing to learn are not willing to change—and if your people aren't willing to change, well then, you might need to change your people.

Without a focus on learning and continuous improvement, team members may become complacent and stagnant in their work. This can lead to a lack of innovation and a decreased ability to respond to new challenges and opportunities. The team won't seek out new or more efficient tools and processes, which will slow down progress towards the team's goals. High performers tend to be active learners; without an environment that fosters that learning, those high performers will leave, hurting the company's ability to compete in the market.

Creating a learning environment is not just about fostering an atmosphere of curiosity and open communication. Being open to learning is just the first step. Actually learning is an active process that requires a few key ingredients to make it happen. Without commitment to the *process* of learning, it's like any other habit; it dies in the graveyard of good intentions.

In his book *Atomic Habits*, James Clear writes: "Your identity emerges out of your habits. Every action is a vote for the type of person you wish to become. No single instance will transform your beliefs, but as the votes build up, so does the evidence of your new identity. This is why habits are crucial. They are the recurring activities that will determine who you are and who you can become."

To become a learning team, your team needs to practice the elements of learning daily: repetition, review, and reflection. These elements are carefully built into Peak by way of the meetings cadence and Team Surveys. Learning is what keeps you on track and continuing to move forward towards your goals and mission; it's part of what makes a team unstoppable.

It's tempting to look at any system or process, as the Future of Work team did, and think, *I can make that more efficient.* But by stripping out the parts of Peak they saw as unnecessary, they actually stripped out one of its most crucial components: the habit-forming that cements learning as a core behavior of the team.

If we think of habits in Charles Duhigg's model from *The Power of Habit*, they follow a repeated formula: Cue, Routine, Reward. Here's how he breaks down this formula:

1. **Cue**: This is a trigger that tells your brain to go into automatic mode, and which habit to use. Cues can be almost anything, from a visual trigger to a time of day, an emotion, a sequence of thoughts, the company of particular people, etc.

2. **Routine:** This can be physical, mental, or emotional. Routines can be incredibly complex or fantastically simple.

3. **Reward:** This helps your brain figure out if this particular loop is worth remembering for the future. Rewards can range from food or drugs that cause physical sensations, to emotional payoffs, such as the feelings of pride that accompany praise or self-congratulation.

You can think of Peak as a system that provides the cue and routine for your team so that they reap the reward almost without thinking about it. What the Future of Work team did was accidentally remove the cue and routine pieces of the formula. Then they wondered why their rewards—better productivity, faster results, smoother workflows, more unity and cohesion as a team—were missing.

PEAK CADENCE

Peak is built on a cadence of meetings that form the backbone for all habit-forming and learning. The particular cadence of Weekly Camp, Quarterly Session, and Annual Session, and the routines built into each of those meetings, ensures the right amount of repetition, review, and reflection to maintain core behaviors like alignment and symbiosis. It forms a rhythm of learning and habit-forming that builds your team behaviors like a muscle without having to expend energy thinking about it.

It's the same concept as trying to build the core behavior of physical fitness in your life. We all know what we need to do to build fitness: exercise, eat well, and sleep well. We also know that leaving those up to chance won't work, or we'd already be doing them. So, what do we do to fix this and get back on course? We form routines that make us *repeat* the actions that build the desired behavior. In other words, we learn the new behavior through repetition.

In the Peak Cadence, your team is practicing the core behaviors of Alignment, Symbiosis, Communication, Empowerment, and Learning through carefully spaced repetition. The process itself is the goal. That's why the system has a cadence, and even the Annual and Quarterly Sessions and Weekly Meetings have a specific format. Each creates cues and routines, and following it creates rewards that make your team lean in further and further. Resist the impulse to streamline the system—doing so blunts its effectiveness and puts your team further away from its reward.

Before walking through the meetings themselves, let's dive into the Team Surveys.

TEAM SURVEYS

A venture-backed team reviewing surveys quarterly is like a group of mountain climbers setting up camps on their ascent up Mount Everest. Just as climbers assess their progress, health, and plan their next move at each camp, the business team uses these quarterly checkpoints to evaluate their performance, make necessary adjustments, and strategize for the coming period. Unpredictable market shifts are akin to unpredictable weather conditions for the climbers—both need to be factored into the plan. These regular assessments are not just formalities, but critical steps on their path to reaching their respective summits.

Any team not devoting time to these key tools of review and assessment is missing out on a massive opportunity to build a culture of accountability. It's the classic saying: "Those who ignore history are doomed to repeat it." You need to identify mistakes, diagnose them, and *agree* on how to avoid them in the future to really learn from them.

The responses on the Team Surveys can sometimes be uncomfortable. There may be areas of disagreement and even conflict. That's okay. In fact, it's an opportunity to build team Symbiosis. In sessions, we set rules around being cognizant of what we say and how we say it. This allows everyone to feel safe in an open and transparent environment. Committing to transparency and vulnerability when discussing issues as a team is a driver of trust, respect, and psychological safety.

The team is also brought closer together through discussing the surveys; they're primarily an opportunity to identify challenges and become better, but they also serve the important function of allowing the team to identify and celebrate wins.

The Annual and Quarterly Peak Team Surveys cover the following areas: People, Review, Planning, OKRs, KPIs, and Team Cadence. The survey is essentially a review of how successful they are at utilizing the tools and building the behaviors throughout the organization. The survey is also a forcing mechanism to get people talking and sharing their thoughts, being heard, *feeling* heard, and setting the team up for the next items on the agenda: Triage discussions and planning.

Here's an example of an Annual Peak Team Survey.

ANNUAL PEAK TEAM SURVEY EXAMPLE

1. Our company mission is clear and fully communicated throughout the organization.

   Disagree 1 2 3 4 5 6 7 8 9 10 *Agree*

2. Our Three Year Vision is clear and fully communicated throughout the organization.

   Disagree 1 2 3 4 5 6 7 8 9 10 *Agree*

3. Our One Year Plan is clear and fully communicated throughout the organization.

Disagree 1 2 3 4 5 6 7 8 9 10 *Agree*

4. Our KPIs (key performance indicators) or metrics are clear and fully communicated throughout the organization.

Disagree 1 2 3 4 5 6 7 8 9 10 *Agree*

5. Our company is using the right KPIs or metrics to measure and lead the business.

Disagree 1 2 3 4 5 6 7 8 9 10 *Agree*

6. What KPIs or metrics should be added, removed, or modified to best lead the business and why?

7. Our OKRs (objectives and key results) last quarter were clear and created focus.

Disagree 1 2 3 4 5 6 7 8 9 10 *Agree*

8. Our OKRs moved the company forward in a positive way this past year.

Disagree 1 2 3 4 5 6 7 8 9 10 *Agree*

9. What were our successes this past year? Why do you consider them a success?

10. What were our misses or failures this past year? Why do you consider them a miss and what was the root cause?

11. Our Weekly Camp Meetings last year were efficient, effective, and well run.

    Disagree 1 2 3 4 5 6 7 8 9 10 *Agree*

12. What issues, roadblocks, or challenges are getting in the way of us successfully achieving our Three Year Vision or One Year Plan?

13. What new opportunities, if taken advantage of, would allow us to successfully achieve our Three Year Vision and One Year Plan?

14. What systems, processes, or technologies would better allow us to successfully achieve our Three Year Vision and One Year Plan?

15. What is our most important issue or challenge that is not being dealt with or difficult to talk about? Why?

16. Our core values are clear and fully communicated throughout the organization.

    Disagree 1 2 3 4 5 6 7 8 9 10 *Agree*

17. We have clear roles and responsibilities throughout the organization.

    Disagree 1 2 3 4 5 6 7 8 9 10 *Agree*

18. We have the right people in the right seats throughout the organization.

    Disagree 1 2 3 4 5 6 7 8 9 10 *Agree*

19. What changes or additions to the org chart do you think would help us achieve our goals? Why?

20. Rate our company culture:

    Poor 1 2 3 4 5 6 7 8 9 10 *Excellent*

21. What are the strengths and weaknesses of our company culture?

22. Reflecting on the survey questions above, what is your top 5% that you believe the company is doing well and the bottom 5% where you believe the company has an opportunity to do better?

Now let's take a deeper look at the Peak Cadence meetings themselves. We've already gone into the Weekly Camp Meeting in depth, so let's dive into the Annual and Quarterly Sessions.

ANNUAL SESSION

For both the Annual and Quarterly Sessions, you'll want to get the right people in the right location for great work to happen. In early stage companies this may be the core team members that represent or lead each functional area of the business; for later stage companies, it's the leadership team that represents each leader representing each of the functional areas of the business. Getting them out of their usual space is best; I encourage offsites. Being in the office puts you in the same mindset as being at work. To open people's minds, it's better to be in a different environment, getting the mental framework unstuck from the day-to-day. A team offsite also provides valuable bonding time, relaxing and having fun together, that is so often overlooked.

Make sure to mark this section, because you'll come back to reference it frequently.

The agenda for the Annual Session is two days, and breaks down as follows.

ANNUAL SESSION AGENDA

Day One

1. Team Connect
2. Session Best Practices
3. Session Expectations
4. Review Roles & Responsibilities
5. Review Annual Peak Team Survey
6. Triage Discussions
7. Build 3YV
8. Build 1YP

Day Two

1. Build Quarterly Team Objectives
2. Build Quarterly Team Key Results
3. Discuss Quarterly Functional Objectives
4. Review Triage List and To Do List
5. Review Expectations
6. Rate the Session

TEAM CONNECT

The team starts with Best and Thanks, getting everyone participating and present. Crucial for setting up an open and positive mindset and environment! Don't skip these small opportunities to practice connection and bonding with your team.

SESSION BEST PRACTICES

The team will walk through some general best practices for the session such as turning off notifications, being present, and creating an open, equal, transparent environment.

SESSION EXPECTATIONS

Have everyone write down and verbalize what they want to accomplish in the session.

REVIEW ROLES & RESPONSIBILITIES

Each team member comes prepared with their roles and responsibilities, defining their functional area, title, role and top five responsibilities. Each team member verbalizes these to the rest of the team, and clarifying questions are asked.

REVIEW TEAM SURVEY

You want to discuss the results together as a team, rather than the CEO reviewing the surveys ahead of time and simply reporting the results.

TRIAGE DISCUSSIONS

Now, you'll do triage, prioritizing the triage items that should be discussed prior to the planning portion of the session.

BUILD 3YV

Another year down, another peak reached. You're looking three years out, so you have a new Three Year Vision to plan. You'll follow the same process you did when creating your original 3YP—with the added benefit of a year's worth of learning under your belt, so your prediction of where you'll be in three years is likely to be even more precise.

BUILD 1YP

What will success look like by the end of this year? Follow the same 1YP process to map out the team's success measures over the course of the next 12 months.

BUILD QUARTERLY TEAM OBJECTIVES

The team will work together to define their objectives for the coming quarter.

BUILD QUARTERLY TEAM KEY RESULTS

This is *how* your team will accomplish those objectives. (Refer back to Part Three for a refresher on building OKRs.)

DISCUSS QUARTERLY FUNCTIONAL OBJECTIVES

If the team has time in the session, they'll each share their functional objectives for the coming quarter.

REVIEW TRIAGE LIST AND TO DO LIST

The team will take a look at the Triage List and To Do List to remove any items that may have been completed by creating the new OKRs, or resolved in the session. All remaining triage items will remain on the list for the next Weekly Camp Meeting.

REVIEW EXPECTATIONS

The team will then review the expectations they set for the session, making sure everyone has been heard and what they wanted to talk about has been covered. Any items not covered are added to the Triage List.

RATE THE SESSION

As you close the session, everyone gives it a rating, similar to the Weekly Camp Meeting, reinforcing the learning behavior and seeking to make each session better than the last.

QUARTERLY SESSION

As you did with the Annual Session, make sure to mark this section, because you'll come back to reference it frequently.

Before each Quarterly Session, the team will complete a standard set of prep work to make sure the session itself is as productive as possible:

1. **Peak Quarterly Team Survey:** This is similar to the Annual Team Survey, and provides a way for the team to track progress from the baseline set at the Annual Session.

2. **Quarterly Peak Questions:** These are a set of questions that will prepare the team to review their progress on the 1YP and build OKRs for the coming quarter.

It's important that the agenda is communicated and understood prior to the session. You want team members to show up aligned and ready to focus.

QUARTERLY SESSION AGENDA

Morning Session
1. Team Connect
2. Session Best Practices
3. Session Expectations
4. Review Quarterly Peak Team Survey
5. Review Current 1YP
6. Triage Discussions

Afternoon Session
1. Build Quarterly Team Objectives
2. Build Quarterly Team Key Results
3. Discuss Quarterly Functional Objectives
4. Review Triage List and To Do List
5. Review Expectations
6. Rate the Session

REVIEW CURRENT 1YP

In the Quarterly Session, this acts as alignment reinforcement. Take a look at the current 1YP and see if you're on or off track, and if any adjustments need to be made. Add any potential changes to the Triage List.

LAUNCH SESSION

When you start Peak with your Launch Session, it's best not to overcomplicate it. Focus on this Launch agenda.

LAUNCH SESSION AGENDA

1. Team Connect
2. Session Best Practices
3. Session Expectations

4. Peak Team Launch Survey
5. Build 1YP*
6. Build Quarterly Team Objectives
7. Build Quarterly Team Key Results
8. Review Expectations
9. Rate the Session

Reminder: the 1YP you're building here is just planning to the end of the current year.

You're seeing a pattern emerge in the meetings cadence, I hope. They follow a similar process. Yes, the Quarterly and Annual Sessions often happen offsite, and they take the whole day (Quarterly) or two days (Annual). But in every other way, they follow the same pattern as the Weekly Camp Meetings, blown up over a broader time scale.

When it comes to starting with Peak, I'll repeat what I wrote earlier in the book: you don't need to wait until a new year to get started. It is best to start now with a Launch Session; no need to wait.

Leaning into Peak and following the cadence is like putting consistency on autopilot. It takes the stress off the CEO and functional leaders as the team gets locked into a consistent iterative growth process.

The Peak cadence is intentional in its flow and repetition. That repeated process—repetition, review, and reflection—incorporates all the tools we've discussed so far to create a web of habit-forming. Sticking to the cadence takes out the guesswork; the cues and routines are built in for the team, and by going through the same steps in three different zoom levels, they'll build their winning core behaviors without thinking about it.

That's what you want out of any habit: to make your desired behavior effortless.

SEVENTEEN

BACK TO BASICS

"Discipline equals freedom."
–JOCKO WILLINK

T DIDN'T TAKE LONG AT THE ANNUAL SESSION FOR THE Future of Work company to realize where they'd gotten off track. The CEO went ahead and spoke for the team: "We're not getting Peak results because we're not actually *doing* Peak."

Nailed it. "Is it clear now why it's important to stick to the Peak cadence and tools?" I asked. We'd spent the past hour essentially doing a refresher course on everything they'd learned when they first started Peak with me four quarters ago, drilling the concepts and relating them to where they stood today to drive home the point of why we were there in the first place.

They all nodded.

"Awesome. Let's stay the course, then. Slow is smooth, smooth is fast. We're going to go through this Annual Session in the exact structure prescribed—no streamlining, no skipping around or ahead."

We completed the rest of the day's session smoothly, and it was obvious the team was happy to snap back into that familiar groove. That's the thing about healthy habits: when you're practicing the behavior you want to master, it naturally feels good. Going to the gym gives you endorphins and shoots your dopamine through the roof. You just have to commit to the rituals of getting there: putting on your workout clothes, lacing up your shoes, driving to the gym, and walking inside. Often, those steps are way harder than the workout itself. That's why they require commitment; they take willpower and discipline. As a team, though, you have the advantage of shared habit-building in doing the small steps that become big behaviors.

Later the next morning, as we were riding out to snorkel in the bay, the CEO said, "We learned our lesson. Peak was working so well at first, but we just fell off the horse and thought we could keep getting those same results without doing most of the routines that made them happen. Once we stopped at the fast food joint, it was hard to stop."

This time around, I scheduled a quick weekly check-in with the CEO to make sure they stayed on top of the Peak cadence and tools. True to their commitment, they stuck with it. Nobody went rogue. They also subscribed to Peak OS Access to give the entire company a resource for learning and reinforcing the Peak system.

Within just a few weeks, they were seeing a huge turnaround in both results and culture.

- They followed the weekly cadence, which meant that every single week, they followed the repetition-review-reflection cycle and built their learning muscle. With each repetition, that core behavior became more deeply ingrained and automatic.

- Symbiosis ticked up right away with the reintroduction of the Team Connect at the start of every meeting. Far from "meetings fluff", these connection points were critical for building camaraderie and shared understanding of each other as people.

- Rating the meeting at the end of each Weekly Camp allowed them to learn from their own routine and become more effective as they went.

- Finally, the simple act of following the rules in the Weekly Camp Meeting transformed it from a rote rundown of points that could have been an email digest into a productive session that produced real results. They went from talking about the work to *doing* the work. The scores when rating the meeting shot up: "We have so much clarity." "We solve so many issues." "The positive energy and wins are addictive."

The following Quarterly Session was like night and day in terms of team performance, and the Team Surveys reflected the change. Unsurprisingly, having practiced the routines that reinforced learning for 90 days, the Learning score shot up across the team.

Another month went by, and one day, I got a text from the CEO. *Oh boy, here come the panicked texts again*, I thought. But I was pleasantly surprised.

Crazy news, man. That partner that left us? They're back

We picked up a few new partners including one of their competitors, sounds like they had some FOMO

We're going to have to reevaluate our revenue target for end of year, because now we're going to blow past it by September!

See you next quarter. 🤜

CASE STUDY: CREDIT KEY

*I conducted this interview with John Tomich,
the CEO and Co-Founder of Credit Key.*

Startups often take on the personality of the CEO, and that's not always a good thing, especially if you want a balanced team. When I started out as CEO, I recognized some of my own weaknesses. I knew I needed a better way of doing things, especially as we hired more people. It's simple math—with more people comes more complications. The more structured approach of Peak came into the picture at just the right time.

Credit Key isn't my first growth company; in learning from past experience, we were able to avoid some of the pitfalls most newer teams make. For instance, I brought in a senior leadership team much earlier than is typical, and it's served us well. We also brought Peak in because it's a system that continues to make us better quarter after quarter as we grow from stage to stage. We've been working with Jeff as our coach going on four years. Nothing is ever perfect in building a fast growing company, but it's really a choice how well you do it.

Back then, we only had a few engineers; if there wasn't a set plan in place, I'd find myself calling them up and changing priorities on the fly. It was chaos. But after we started with Peak, we started working in two-week sprints, giving everyone clarity and direction.

It's like driving a car: if you only focus on what's directly in front of you, you'll end up crashing. Instead, you need to look ahead, plan, and strategize. The classic startup CEO might be used to changing directions at a whim, but as your company grows, structure, consistency, and discipline become crucial.

One of the best things about working with Peak was how quickly we saw results. Our teams instantly became more productive; it was obvious to everyone in the company. And, despite our limited resources and growing from a dozen to sixty employees, we've consistently achieved our goals. In the tech world, you hear a lot of stories of companies cutting down their workforce without any drop in output. That kind of inefficiency is what we're trying to avoid. We want to stay agile and focused.

Peak, and especially the resources the whole team has access to on Peak OS Access, has been instrumental in our growth. I can't imagine running our current organization without this discipline, focus, and efficiency that comes from Peak.

CONCLUSION

SCALING THE MOUNTAIN

Before you put this book down and start planning your Peak Launch Session, there's one more quick thing I want you to absorb.

And, if you're eagle-eyed or acronym-happy like I am, this may be something you noticed with mounting frustration while reading (although my editor reassures me that the majority of you likely didn't clock it).

The core team behaviors that created the backbone of this book, and that mean the difference between success and failure for VC-backed companies, are Alignment, Symbiosis, Communication, Empowerment, and Learning.

I presented them in that order because it was the best way to communicate and build on the concepts and tools that create

Peak. But when I hand out reference materials at conferences, when I put together the Peak OS Access knowledge base, and when I present Peak to teams for the first time at their Launch Sessions, I use a handy acronym for these behaviors: *SCALE*.

- Symbiosis
- Communication
- Alignment
- Learning
- Empowerment

So, apologies for the easter egg, but now that you know Peak like the back of your hand (right?), you can move forward with that handy mnemonic device, and adopt it as your mindset going forward.

SCALE. That's what we're after; reaching for not just the closest peak, but the *highest* peak. Building to scale: setting up the organization so it can grow rapidly without rearchitecting over and over. Reaching for not just profitability, but for a massive return on investment, a huge exit at the end of years of the hard work you and your team have dedicated yourselves to.

An exit, for example, like the one achieved by the FinTech company from Part Two: Alignment. After running Peak, they recently enjoyed a 10x exit.

Building an unstoppable team is the difference between success and failure. And it's a choice. It can't be left to chance or assumption. It's something that must be actively chosen day in and day out.

Teams that win demonstrate core behaviors—behaviors that are non-negotiable. It's important to understand that winning this game isn't a "best out of three" situation. You need to have all five SCALE behaviors to get to the summit as a team. And if you choose to work on them, if you choose to commit to the system of habits that will build those behaviors, your team will become unstoppable.

Committing to Peak doesn't require a ton of extra work. In fact, it's less work. It does require consistency, though; it's not an a la carte menu. If you're feeling strong about some of the tools and habits you learned in this book, but shaky on others, continue to reread or re-listen to this book or, head over to collective-genius.com to get your Peak OS Access subscription going, get set up with your Peak Coach, and become one of our Peak Teams.

Peak is about drilling the fundamentals, building the habits that create winning behaviors. These fundamentals are repetitive, methodical—and absolutely crucial.

Remember: fundamentals win championships. I'll repeat that Bruce Lee quote: "I fear not the man who has practiced 10,000 kicks once, but I fear the man who has practiced one kick 10,000 times." The words *Bruce Lee* and *fear* in the same sentence really underlines the power of mastering the fundamentals, and that's the whole purpose of Peak.

As founders, we're driven to take a path others haven't taken. To build and create the unthinkable. To succeed against all odds. That's who we are; that's what propels us forward.

We're driven to create and go beyond—and with our success, we drive the world forward. Your success isn't just important to your investors; it's important to everyone.

Keep climbing, my friends. Never, never, never stop climbing.

Take the Peak Teams Assessment

Ready to see where your team stands right now, and start to plan your roadmap to the summit? Head over to collective-genius.com/peak -teams-assessment *to take the Peak Teams Assessment and get started.*

ACKNOWLEDGMENTS

To my wife Anna: you make me a better person every day. Thank you for doing everything you do and for the sacrifices and contributions you made to help me bring this book project to life. Always better together. Love you and thank you.

Thank you to my kids for being flexible—from my time away working, to waiting in the car, to letting me "finish one more thing" before we go.

Thank you to my parents Paul and Carole Martin for always giving me everything you could without hesitation to encourage every interest I've ever had. You also helped me master the fundamentals: mom taught me how to organize, dad taught me business. Absolutely grateful. Thank you.

Thank you to my brother Pat for teaching me the importance of sports and teamwork.

To my entire family, and in particular my uncles Jay, Ed, and Craig: thank you for indulging my relentless curiosity about business and entrepreneurship throughout my youth.

Thank you to all our Peak Teams, Venture Partners, and Collective Genius team members throughout the years. Especially Geoff Grcevich, who has always been steadfast in this journey together.

And to all the people that provided the Peak Team stories for the book: Melanie Stricklan, John Tomich, Anne Hallock, Ryan Broshar, Anand Shah, Adam Weber, John Bertrand, and Keith Lauver, and in memory of Bobby Crumpton.

Thank you to the fellow authors who provided me invaluable guidance through the book-writing journey: Brad Feld and Amos Schwartzfarb.

Finally, thank you to Meghan McCracken, without whom this book would not have come to fruition.

ABOUT THE AUTHOR

Over the course of a two-decade career, Jeff James Martin has worked with hundreds of venture-backed leadership teams, from seed to exit, and investors across the US and worldwide. Jeff has personally founded, sold, and played multiple roles at venture-backed technology companies. In 2004, Jeff founded Collective Genius to assist CEOs, founders, and investors to build high-performing teams. As a mentor to accelerator programs and a go-to for VC firms' portfolio companies globally, Jeff has become a sought-after speaker worldwide. Jeff lives in Los Angeles with his wife and five kids, where he teaches and competes in Brazilian jiu-jitsu as a black belt and coaches high school athletics.

www.ingramcontent.com/pod-product-compliance
Lightning Source LLC
Chambersburg PA
CBHW030459210326
41597CB00013B/730